THE BATTLE OF ALBUERA 1811

THE BATTLE OF ALBUERA 1811

'Glorious Field of Grief'

by

Michael Oliver
and Richard Partridge

Pen & Sword
MILITARY

First published in Great Britain in 2007 by
Pen & Sword Military
an imprint of
Pen & Sword Books Ltd
47 Church Street
Barnsley
South Yorkshire
S70 2AS

ISBN 978 1 84415 461 6

A CIP catalogue record for this book is
available from the British Library

Typeset in Sabon by
Phoenix Typesetting, Auldgirth, Dumfriesshire

Printed and bound in England by
Biddles Ltd, King's Lynn

Pen & Sword Books Ltd incorporates the Imprints of Pen & Sword
Aviation, Pen & Sword Maritime, Pen & Sword Military, Wharncliffe
Local History, Pen & Sword Select, Pen & Sword Military Classics and
Leo Cooper.

For a complete list of Pen & Sword titles please contact
PEN & SWORD BOOKS LIMITED
47 Church Street, Barnsley, South Yorkshire, S70 2AS, England
E-mail: enquiries@pen-and-sword.co.uk
Website: www.pen-and-sword.co.uk

Contents

List of Plates

Plates are found between pp. 112 and 113.

List of Maps

Acknowledgements

We have received assistance from numerous people and organizations in doing our research on this book and that help has been invaluable. So our thanks go to members of the 'Napoleon Series' internet group, the hospitable people of the village of Albuera – particularly Macarena, who looks after the Information Centre – the monks at Ciudad Rodrigo seminary, who allowed us access to a full set of pristine first edition volumes of Toreno and asked us to talk to their young students about the Peninsular War. Thirty years ago, Michael Oliver wrote a manuscript about Albuera for another publisher but publication was cancelled due to the 1974 miners' strike. The research done at that time was useful in seeing this current version complete and we must thank the then Lt Col Chard of the Fusilier Brigade for allowing Mike access to the regimental records and a sight of the contents of the 'Albuera Chest'.

In particular, we would like to thank Mark S Thompson whose book *The Fatal Hill* was an inspiration when we visited the battlefield and afterwards. We contacted Mark and have had several illuminating exchanges with him. He has provided copies of several original documents without demur and was kind enough to cast his eye over our manuscript before publication. We share his mystification as to the reasons for the absence of General Madden during the battle and wonder whether an explanation will ever surface.

Sr Miguel Angel Martin Mas, expert on the Battle of Salamanca, author of a number of excellent publications on Napoleonic troops and the War of Independence and curator of the Museum at Los Arapiles has assisted us in his typical unstinting manner. He accompanied us on three of our visits to

Spain, organized our hotels and transport and opened many doors to relevant facilities we had not even dreamed existed – including the council offices at Bailén where some magnificent paintings of the war hang – and the Ciudad Rodrigo seminary. He has assisted with translations, arranged meetings and is now a great friend.

Sr Jesús Maroto, who wrote the Introduction to this book for our potential Spanish readers, plied us with copies of original manuscripts and maps from Spanish and French archives, profiles of some of the Spanish generals and memoirs and reports from people we had not appreciated had written about their experiences – among them Jean-Baptiste Heralde, the French surgeon-general. Sr Maroto is doing a considerable amount of work in Spain to rekindle interest in their military heritage generally and the War of Independence in particular.

The maps have been provided by Cartography Services (www.cartography-services.co.uk).

Finally we would like to acknowledge the generosity of the family of the late Hugh Lambrick who sadly passed away before his own work on Albuera could be published. His research was made available to us and assisted in our work. The family is planning to have his book published on the internet and we believe it will be at www.lambrick.co.uk. It covers a wider canvas and gives a fuller examination of Sir William Beresford and the Badajoz campaign than is intended in this history.

This book is dedicated to all who lost their lives at or because of the Battle of Albuera. Most did not find marked graves, many were far from their homes; to some, Albuera was their home but denied to them through no fault of their own.

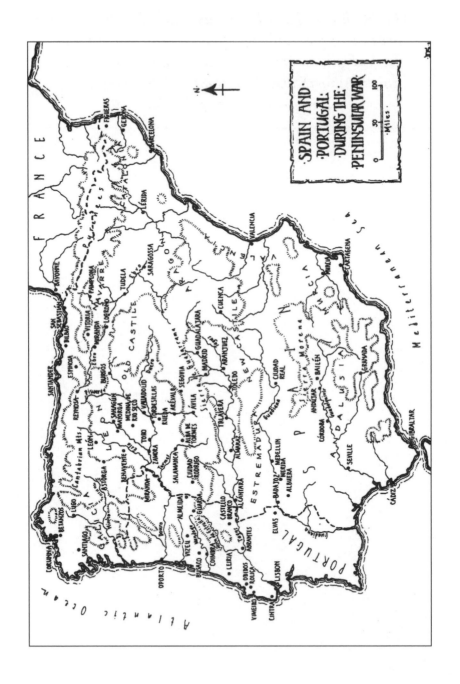

SPAIN AND
PORTUGAL
DURING THE
PENINSULAR WAR

Three hosts combine to offer sacrifice;
Three tongues prefer strange orisons on high;
Three gaudy standards flout the pale blue skies;
The shouts are France, Spain, Albion, Victory!
The foe, the victim, and the fond ally
That fights for all, but ever fights in vain,
Are met – as if at home they could not die –
To feed the crow on Talavera's plain,
And fertilize the field that each pretends to gain.

There shall they rot – Ambition's honour'd fools!
Yes, Honour decks the turf that wraps their clay!
Vain Sophistry! in these behold the tools,
The broken tools, that tyrants cast away
By myriads, when they dare to pave their way
With human hearts – to what? – a dream alone.
Can despots compass aught that hails their sway?
Or call with truth one span of earth their own,
Save that wherein at last they crumble bone by bone?

Oh, Albuera! glorious field of grief!
As o'er thy plain the Pilgrim prick'd his steed,
Who could foresee thee, in a space so brief,
A scene where mingling foes should boast and bleed!
Peace to the perish'd! may the warrior's meed
And tears of triumph their rewards prolong!
Till others fall where other chieftains lead
Thy name shall circle round the gaping throng,
And shine in worthless lays, the theme of transient song!

(Lord Byron, *Childe Harold's Pilgrimage*,
stanzas XLI to XLIII)

THE BATTLE OF
ALBUERA 1811

Introduction*

Jesús Maroto

An important highway, N-432, takes vehicles that leave the city of Badajoz by a route that passes near the locality of Albuera. If the traveller is driving quickly, he will probably not notice a mural at the entrance to the village on which can be read the first verse of a poem by Lord Byron: 'Oh Albuera, Glorious Field of Grief!' In the same place one can see, in addition, an effigy of four soldiers: a Spaniard, a Briton, a Portuguese and a Frenchman. Underneath each one of them, in the language of his nationality, the inscription continues: 'In rows, just as they fought, they lay like hay in the open countryside . . .'

On the other hand, if the traveller is curious and crosses the road with the thought of discovering new places, the sight of so particular a mural will surely make him stop his vehicle and enter the streets of the town. In the main square his curiosity will be further aroused when approaching a commemorative monument of the battle that was fought in the fields nearby on 16 May 1811: a pedestal crowned by a bust of General Castaños, the victor of another battle which happened three years before – the famous Battle of Bailén. To each side of the bust, two small columns are raised on whose bases the names of several allied generals appear: Blake, Lardizabal, Ballesteros, Zayas, Carlos de España and Penne

---

*Authors' note: We asked Sr Maroto to write this introduction in Spanish after all the assistance he provided in obtaining Spanish and French archival material. He is a much respected historian and leading member of the Forum for the Study of Spanish Military History. It was his opinion that the book would be of great interest to the Spanish reader of military history and we believed it would be helpful for such readers to have an introduction in their own language. This is an abridged translation of Jesús' words. The full Spanish text appears as Appendix 3.

for Spain; Beresford, Hamilton, Lumley, Cole, Stewart and Alten for Britain and Portugal.

Outside the little village is a small obelisk that commemorates fallen Spanish officers of the General Staff in the battle; another memorial – rather larger and of more recent construction – remembers the British dead. In addition, next to the church is a centre interpreting the battle that, by means of a diorama and diverse maps and engravings, gives an account of all that occurred in the fields of Albuera that tragic day in 1811. In the display cabinets are different objects found by farmers when working the fields – projectiles, clasps, buckles, fragments of sabres and muskets – that can produce a shiver that accompanies the visitor for many hours after leaving the place.

Every year, towards the middle of May, several thousand people – up to 20,000 on occasion – go to the village to experience the spectacle of a recreation of the battle. Volunteers come from different countries and join the greater part of the inhabitants of Albuera, for a few days becoming soldiers of the time of the Napoleonic wars; they march, shoot and mount fearsome cavalry charges. This event, incorporated in 1965, lasts three days and has grown to about nine hundred participants on the battlefield. In addition, about three hundred neighbours present a play with the title 'Albuera: history of love and death'. People who are present at these activities soon come to realize that this is not a celebration, but the commemoration of an event of the past that caused the small town of Badajoz to enter the history of Europe. Everyone that has been present at re-enactments of this type knows the objective: to recall past battles and conflicts so that such errors are not committed again; to promote friendship between towns and to teach history by means of making that history accessible.

Amongst the public, some will identify with one side or the other or perhaps a military unit that fascinates them. However, between the re-enactors it matters little what a frightening Polish lancer or a soldier of the British Middlesex regiment imagines about killing an enemy in the battle because, at the end of the day, everyone will gather in Wellington Park[1] to pay tribute to the fallen of the Battle of Albuera.

At this point, I would expect to be asked what Albuera repre-

sents for Spaniards interested in the history of the War of
Independence. It is important to recognize that, although several
articles in specialized magazines have been published, a deep study
of the battle has still not been published in Spain. However, in the
United Kingdom, several works do exist. You have in your hands
the third or fourth. However, in our country, there are several dedicated to Bailén and, in lesser amounts, to the Battles of Talavera
and of the Arapiles (Salamanca), as well as isolated works dedicated to the Battles of Barrosa, Ocaña and Sagunto, and that these
two last, as is well known, were two catastrophic battles for the
Spanish armies involved.

The Battle of Albuera was the fourth battle in which the Spanish
and British armies participated as allies. In the first of the previous
occasions, the soldiers of Sir John Moore saw the rest of the army
of the Marques Romana marching after them in the tragic retreat
towards La Coruña, soon to end up losing sight of them in the
mountain ranges of Galicia. Spanish armies, comprising sick and
inadequately uniformed soldiers, gave a poor impression to their
British companions. One such was a Spanish army that had
suffered a resounding defeat in the battle of Espinosa de los
Monteros. At first it was formed from trained soldiers, but after
the fiasco of the battle and several days of a terrible retreat through
the mountains of the northern Peninsula, they thought only about
surviving and fleeing as far as possible from the lethal French
cavalry. In addition, to further demoralize these troops, the news
arrived that two other Spanish armies had been defeated at Tudela
and Gamonal. After the eventual evacuation of the British troops
from the ports of La Coruña and Vigo, any allied nation would
have sued for peace because, technically, Spain had already lost the
war. However the Spanish continued resisting, and this would offer
new opportunities to fight again shoulder to shoulder with the
British.

The second encounter took place at Talavera. New units had
been created and combined with the remnants of the old ones and,
once more, Spaniards took themselves to the battlefield. One army,
that of Extremadura, under the command of General Cuesta, was
united to Sir Arthur Wellesley's British force. However, morale
could not be very high among men who had been defeated and who

had seen so many of their comrades desert. In addition, they lacked training. At Talavera, the main weight of the French attack fell on the well-trained British troops. At the same time, several battalions of inexperienced Spanish troops fled when hearing the roar caused by the firing of muskets coming from their own side. Although Cuesta severely punished those who were apprehended, some even with death, the impression that this episode caused among the British troops could not have been worse. Spain had not been able to provide promised food and transport to the British army; if the Spaniards were additionally untrustworthy on the battlefield, it made little sense for the British army to remain in Spain. Logically, Wellesley decided to retire to Portugal to put his men, who now faced a massive advance from three French armies converging on the allies, out of danger. Despite the victory achieved, everything was a disaster. Bitterness seized the hearts of British officers, who lamented that so little came out of that campaign after so many sacrifices. From their point of view, the Spanish were cowardly and took advantage of British heroism. However, from the Spanish point of view, the British had left their allies to meet the unstoppable advance of the more numerous and much better quality armies of the French.

In the previous year, the somewhat fortunate victory at Bailén acted as a mirage that fooled the Spanish Central Junta into believing they would be able to repeat that campaign, which had caused the evacuation of Madrid by the French. The result was very different when everything ended in a great defeat for Spain at the Battle of Ocaña. This was a disaster of enormous proportions that brought about the destruction of the Spanish Central Armies. Spain appeared to lose the war for the second time. Many Spaniards therefore capitulated and gave a great reception to King Joseph Bonaparte in a triumphal trip through Andalusia. In the south, Cádiz was left as a lone bastion of resistance and everything indicated that it would end up surrendering to Marshal Victor. The only alternative many veteran soldiers had was to join the guerrilla bands which were being created. Small groups of officers of the Spanish army thought that long-term resistance could end in victory. But such a victory would be very distant if it were not possible to count on British aid.

Introduction

Surprisingly, Cádiz resisted the besieging French. After a time, the British decided that it could be worth the trouble to collaborate with the Spaniards and try to raise the siege which the troops of Marshal Victor were prosecuting. This was the third attempt at Hispano-British collaboration which culminated in the Battle of Barrosa (or Chiclana, as it is called by the Spanish). This battle was fought a year after the beginning of the siege of Cádiz. Two Spanish divisions and one Anglo-Portuguese participated and the battle was decided in favour of the allies, although the victory itself went to the Anglo-Portuguese division that, in fact, faced very superior forces. The Spaniards did not help them with all the forces which they had, but limited themselves to restoring communications with Cádiz, following the instructions of General La Peña. British officers accused the Spaniards of treason and the Central Junta decided to dismiss the Spanish general. Resentment between both parties was increased with this painful episode. The Spanish could not this time blame the British for lack of aid, since the Battle of Barrosa rather showed the opposite. And what is worse, these Spanish troops had received effective training. It was not about inexperienced soldiers, but men trained very well by Generals Zayas and Lardizábal in the field of San José – see Appendix 2. The year of 1811 began with British and Spaniards sending each other continuous reproaches and accusations that each had caused the delicate situation in which they found themselves: Spanish incompetence, according to the British, and British lack of collaboration, according to the Spanish. But another, fourth opportunity of collaboration was to present itself and this occurred with Albuera.

The battle cannot be summarized more skilfully than is described in the following pages – the fruit of the investigations of Michael Oliver and Richard Partridge. Their description is so detailed and interesting, it allows us to become spectators, so that our imagination conjures up the images of that event. These pages must be read like a novel. There was disagreement among the participants, there were heroes, difficult terrain, sacrifice . . . In summary, it must also be said that there is a great diversity of opinions, stories and descriptions. There were clouds caused by gunpowder that flooded the battlefield; rain that prevented identification when troops encountered one another; riders armed with lances who arose as if from the mist and who, in the beginning, seemed to be Spanish cavalry but soon turned out to be the terrifying Poles led by Colonel Konovka. Nonetheless, Michael Oliver and Richard Patridge have been able to write a great story of total historical reliability.

Was the Battle of Albuera able to eliminate part of the lack of understanding that existed then between Spaniards and British? Almost certainly not. Moyle Sherer tells that, when Zayas's men were relieved to retire behind the 2nd Division: 'a noble Spanish officer rode towards me, and addressed me with pride and brave anxiety that he had ordered his soldiers to retire, but that they were not fleeing'. It would still be some time before Arthur Wellesley was named commander-in-chief of the Allied armies; in that interval, the lack of understanding between the two parties would be reduced, because the Duke's cautious and measured approach would prevail over the anxiety of the Spaniards to free their country of the French. Spain had come close to losing the war. The glacial blue stare of a Grandee of Spain, Sir Arthur Wellesley, was to become embedded in the memory of all the Spanish generals who fought under his orders. If we contemplate the picture that Goya painted, the hardness of his gaze still shakes us.

It is a relief that the authors of this work of investigation have considered the documentation gathered in the Spanish archives. As Spaniards we must collaborate with British historians dedicated to the study of the Peninsular War, because this way we will be able to understand different points of view about a conflict of, in many ways, such difficult interpretation. I hope that this book contributes to increase the collaboration between historians of both countries, in such a way we can overcome old historical quarrels and admit that thousands of British soldiers gave their life for the independence of Spain. This country has begun to recognize the merits of their British allies with more and more numerous monuments, but these are still insufficient.

Albuera is only a beginning. It is certain that there will be commemorations of the bicentennial of the beginning of the War of Independence that I hope will bear a great deal of fruit.

Chapter One

Napoleonic Warfare
and the Peninsular War

Background

The War in the Iberian Peninsula, between 1808 and 1814, was described to us once, by a Spaniard, as three simultaneous wars. First, the war known in Britain as 'The Peninsular War' was a conflict in which a British expeditionary field army, much of her navy and a goodly portion of her gold, went to help the beleaguered Spanish and Portuguese people throw off the yoke of a foreign invader. Second, it was a Spanish and Portuguese War of Independence – indeed, it was known to the Spanish as 'La Guerra de la Independencia' – those prosecuting the fight being, first and foremost, the civil population rather than the respective governments and, finally, at least for the Spanish, it encompassed a civil war – *Patriotistas* against *Afrancesados*. It certainly represented many things to many nations: to the British it was largely a means of stopping Napoleon's expansionism and overcoming his 'Continental System' of trade embargoes whilst, to the French and their emperor, it was a further conflict that would consummate their conquest of Europe. To much of the rest of Europe, it was a hope that someone was prosecuting a second front to distract Napoleon from his designs on their own independence. Whatever the aims and objects of the various governments and rulers, to the soldiers who fought it, regardless of nationality, it was a bloody and seemingly interminable war fought without the 'gentility' of the conflicts of a hundred years previously.

The Spanish Bourbon royal household suffered internal division and much of the government was undertaken by Manuel Godoy, the Queen's favourite, otherwise known as 'El Principe de la Paz'. King Carlos IV, whilst vacillating over Godoy's attempted reforms of the army, was at loggerheads with his son, Ferdinand, and Ferdinand would have nothing to do with Godoy who might otherwise have achieved some improvements with his proposed reforms. Typically, Napoleon Bonaparte saw his chance of exploiting this tortured situation for his own ends.

Portugal was generally a weak nation and Spain had its own designs against its ruling house of Braganza. The military establishments of neither of the two states could be described as efficient or modern, having their organizations rooted in the Frederician tradition of tightly disciplined and highly drilled units that developed in Europe's armies from the 1740s on, but which were found wanting by the new mobility practised by the French revolutionary troops of th 1790s. Using this disunity to dupe the Spanish royal family into accepting his assistance (Carlos believed the French emperor would help him with his designs on Portugal) Napoleon arranged to insert large numbers of troops into Spain and for the differences between Carlos and Ferdinand to culminate in the abdication of the former and effective kidnap of the latter. Godoy became, for a time at least, a willing puppet of the emperor but, having disposed of Spain's rulers, Napoleon proclaimed his brother Joseph as king and, in a series of almost bloodless coups, had French military commanders take over many of the key cities and fortresses that had not already succumbed.

He had, it would appear, underestimated the nature and mood of the Spanish people as a whole, however. On 2 May 1808 simultaneous riots in various cities resulted in the deaths of a number of French soldiers and high-ranking Spaniards suspected – often wrongly – of collaboration. Joachim Murat, the colourful French marshal who had been appointed to administer the country until Joseph Bonaparte was formally enthroned, turned a battery of guns upon the rioters in Madrid and gave them the infamous 'whiff of grapeshot' that the citizens of Paris had experienced many years earlier. This had the dual effect of quelling the immediate disturbances but creating the festering sore which Napoleon later referred to as 'the Spanish ulcer'.

With the energetic participation of the clergy in various parts of Spain and Portugal, the populace was roused to open resistance and the long struggle for independence had begun. Untrained bands of peasants gathered in the mountains and, armed only with farm implements and fowling pieces, preyed on any straggling French soldiery unfortunate enough to become separated from its parent unit. Portugal, encouraged by the Spanish example and the departure of their own royal family for Brazil, followed suit. Britain offered assistance, both financial and military, which was accepted by the new Portuguese authorities (in the form of the Bishop of Oporto and the *junta* he led), whilst Spain embraced the offer of gold and materiel but eschewed the offer of a British expeditionary force – at least in the early days of the war.

The French laid siege to two of the cities they had not occupied (Zaragoza and Valencia) but the citizens and some regular military units organized by a few energetic leaders (among them Don José Palafox and Don José Caro) resisted. In Zaragoza, Palafox held the French at bay for many weeks and Caro at Valencia was, after a comparatively short siege, left alone by Marshal Moncey who was called to another part of the country. These two cities became an example to the rest of Spain as to the effectiveness of resistance against the usurpers. Any citizen not enthusiastically participating in such resistance was dealt with rapidly and summarily by his fellows. Gradually, local *juntas* formed and the old Spanish provinces re-emerged with governments and military establishments: Andalucía, León, Castile, Galicia, Aragón, Catalonia and others formed their own armies and objectives but no overall ruling power coordinated the efforts of the Spanish insurrection. Indeed, the provinces renewed old enmities and jealousies and many individuals in government lined their pockets with the largesse bestowed by Britain to the ultimate detriment of the country.[1] Even after the formation of a central *junta*, the bickering continued.

Spain had a regular army and parts of it had the necessary training to be effective in a properly directed military effort.

However, the most effective parts had been cleverly dispersed by the French emperor. A large corps, under the Marqués de la Romana, had been in Denmark, 'assisting' the French (in reality, they had been removed as a danger to French designs in Spain) and were 'detained' once the insurrections commenced at home. Smaller groupings were directed to the French campaign against Portugal, where they could be watched and, if need arose, neutralized by those French corps with whom they cooperated. Nevertheless, as the French design became clear, several Spanish generals acted promptly and their forces were placed at the disposal of the new provincial authorities. These bodies became nuclei around which larger armies could be formed. Regrettably, all but a few of the levies who flocked to the colours were banded into new units rather than being allocated to the old regular regiments where they would have been gradually assimilated. The new infantry regiments lacked training, and in many cases even arms, so when called upon to fight did not show the steadiness of the more established formations. Cavalry horses were in short supply and this arm of the Spanish military seldom performed or even behaved with distinction. The artillery, by comparison, were well-trained, fairly well-supplied with equipment and, in most respects, the equal of their counterparts in any army.

Portugal, in contrast, had had its army disbanded by the French governor, General Andoche Junot, in 1807. New units formed around some old cadres but these became the equivalent of raw battalions, whose ranks were filled with levies, and the country did not progress much from this state until the appointment, in 1809, of a British commander (the very same man who later commanded the allies at Albuera – Sir William Carr Beresford), with the rank of Portuguese marshal, to reorganize and retrain the army.

The involvement of Britain did not occur in any serious form until some weeks after the insurrection had commenced. Britain offered assistance to Spain but the new Spanish order judged itself capable of armed resistance of a sufficient nature to be up to defeating the enemy. However, it accepted financial assistance and arms from its recent foe – Britain and Spain had been officially at war since 1804, which was largely due to the latter's alliance with

France, although battles had been exclusively naval. Despite the peace which was declared, Spain would not countenance the arrival of a British expeditionary force on its shores. Petty rivalry and jealousies bedevilled the Spanish cause and even the assistance given by Britain was misappropriated and wasted in many instances. It must also be said that Britain did not use the most sensible or efficient means of distributing its aid, much of the responsibility for this falling on inadequate individual 'agents', many of whose only claim to suitability was – as Sir William Napier intimates[2] – their knowledge of the Spanish language.

Consequently, the first Spanish actions against French troops were almost entirely their own efforts and met with mixed results. Britain and Portugal, however, acted in concert and, eventually, produced a highly effective partnership. In the initial encounters, Portugal's contribution was minor but once Beresford's efforts began to make themselves felt Portuguese troops made contributions to the Allied effort of no small importance.

The War up to 15 May 1811

The first real battle between French and Spanish troops was at Medina de Rioseco on 14 July 1808 and here a smaller but infinitely more experienced and better quality French army beat a Spanish force that political intriguing had reduced in strength and dissipated across the countryside it traversed to reach the battlefield. There were, however, some early signs of a Spanish army's ability to soak up damage and re-emerge, shortly after being beaten and dispersed, with renewed belief in itself. Just five days after Medina de Rioseco and some hundreds of kilometres south at Bailén, the first French invasion of Andalucía was crushed by a mixture of Spanish self-belief, French ineptitude and sheer blind luck. The news of the Spanish victory, however, echoed around Europe like distant thunder. This news not only encouraged the Spanish people to flock to the colours, but strengthened Britain's belief in their decision to intervene and reassured other European nations that the second front might have some teeth.

The lack of a central government in Spain led to parochialism and a ruinous absence of coordination. Rather than appoint one of the provincial captains-general to command all Spain's armies and carry through a national strategy, the *juntas* formulated their own local strategies and appointed general officers – often of dubious capabilities – to command the armies raised to carry them out. Francisco Castaños, the commander-in-chief of the victorious army at Bailén, although not the ablest and most charismatic of commanders, had the confidence of his troops and the formal training at least to have the theoretical qualifications to wield overall command. Sadly, following its victory, his army was broken up, a substantial proportion under the Swiss general, Teodoro Reding, being sent east to Catalonia to form the nucleus of resistance to French depredations in that province. Castaños himself continued to command one of the provincial armies but this had been filled out with raw recruits and little training was undertaken.

When Sir Arthur Wellesley landed his army over the surf of Mondego Bay in Portugal in the fierce heat of an Iberian summer, he was met by a Portuguese 'army', more than two-thirds of which was indifferently armed peasantry, commanded by General Bernardino Freire. After supplying 5,000 muskets to Freire's army, Wellesley was invited to join the Portuguese general on an ill-advised march into the interior. The Portuguese had no supplies to feed even their own army, so Wellesley preferred to remain on the coast, where he could obtain what he needed from the navy who maintained a strong presence off-shore. The two generals fell out over this and, as a result, the British proceeded southwards alone. They defeated a portion of Junot's army at Roliça (Obidos) and continued southwards. At Vimeiro, Junot attacked the British in a strong position and was comprehensively defeated. Wellesley had, some time earlier, been superseded by two more senior generals, Burrard and Dalrymple, who following the battle negotiated surrender terms so advantageous to the French that they and Wellesley were recalled to England to explain their actions. Sir John Moore, recently returned from Sweden, was appointed, in place of his three predecessors, to command of the British army. He was probably the most able of the British generals of the time with the exception of Wellesley himself. In August 1808, the same month in which Wellesley ended the

French occupation of Portugal, the Spanish established the Central Junta, a body which had a legitimate claim to act as the government of Spain and had the, albeit grudging, support of the local *juntas*.

It was agreed that Moore would cooperate with the two Spanish armies, under Castaños and Blake (one of the generals commanding at Medina de Rioseco), established and coordinated by the Central Junta in their effort to defeat the French on the line of the Ebro River in northern Spain. The French army, however, was being greatly reinforced and Napoleon himself was on his way to take command and deal once and for all with the troublesome Spaniards. Accordingly, Moore put his army on the march to take his place in the great line, little suspecting that the Spanish armies would have been beaten and scattered by the emperor long before he arrived. Then isolated and alone, Moore determined to remove his precious command – the only field army which Britain could deploy – from danger, by taking them back to Britain. But first he bought some time for the citizens of Madrid, who were preparing to defend their city from seizure and occupation, simultaneously demonstrating that the British army was a force to be reckoned with. In a brilliant feat, British cavalry under Sir Edward Paget destroyed a regiment of French chasseurs at Benavente and stung the French into pursuing Moore's army to the far north-western corner of the Peninsula in the depths of a fierce Iberian winter. Moore successfully organized the withdrawal of his army but was fatally injured in the final battle at La Coruña. His adversary, Marshal Soult, together with a substantial force, was effectively lost to the French for weeks as a result. Although Madrid fell to the French emperor, the reputation of the British had been salvaged along with a substantial part of her army which would live to fight another day.

Fortunately for the future of British arms in the Peninsula, Wellesley was exonerated from blame over the terms of the French capitulation after Vimeiro, whilst his two superiors were censured but treated leniently. Wellesley returned to Portugal having expressed the opinion that the country – or at least the key area around Lisbon – could be successfully defended and any invading French army held at bay long enough and at sufficient cost to itself to render such an invasion ineffective and doomed to failure. The means to achieve this were immediately set in motion on Wellesley's arrival in the form of the construction of a series of forts, field works and defensive positions in the area of Torres Vedras, together with contingency plans for a form of scorched-earth arrangements whereby the peasants in the vicinity would destroy all means by which an invading French army might sustain itself in the field. Simultaneously, General Beresford began his reforms of the Portuguese army.

In March 1809, Marshal Soult had journeyed southwards and reoccupied Oporto in the north of Portugal and Marshal Victor was preparing to march westwards from Mérida. Losing no time, Wellesley moved against Soult and, by a clever subterfuge using wine barges to transfer his men across the wide Douro River, coordinated with a determined out-flanking march by Beresford, crossed the river before Soult could react and compromised his situation so effectively that the marshal was forced to retire by mountain paths, leaving all his artillery, stores and materiel behind. His force only escaped capture by the speed of its retreat and a certain dilatoriness in the pursuit by Portuguese troops and some militia detailed to cut a river crossing which Soult had to use. Meanwhile, Victor had moved from Mérida and Wellesley had to abandon the pursuit and return south. However, this turned out to be merely a reconnaissance in force and came to nothing. Significantly, this pursuit was made with single Portuguese battalions included in British brigades for the first time and the measure proved highly successful.

After a month of rest, resupply and recuperation, the British commenced offensive manoeuvres against Victor in which Wellesley was to cooperate with the elderly Spanish General Gregorio de la Cuesta. Cuesta was undoubtedly brave and had achieved substantial successes against the French revolutionary armies in the Pyrenees at the end of the previous century. However, he was over 70 years old, suspicious of Wellesley, who was being proposed as a potential generalissimo of the Spanish army (a position which Cuesta may well have had designs on himself) and very infirm, having been ridden over by his own retreating cavalry at the Battle of Medellin some weeks earlier.

There appears to have been some difficulty, therefore, in the two commanders reaching agreement on the manner and scope of their cooperation. Additionally, promised supplies had not materialized and both armies were suffering from a lack of food.

Eventually, agreement was reached and the two armies commenced a march towards Talavera de la Reina, a small town on the river Tagus. In order to prevent the two French corps of Victor and King Joseph Bonaparte from combining with a third under General Sebastiani, Cuesta had been given authority to issue orders to a second Spanish army under General Venegas to manoeuvre so that Sebastiani would be forced to watch him rather than join Joseph and Victor. Sadly this plan failed completely and the Allied army was finally faced by the combined French army in its entirety.

The Battle of Talavera proper was fought on 28 July. During the previous night, the French had mounted an attack which caught the Allies unaware and almost resulted in disaster for them. Fortunately, the situation was restored and, the following morning, repeated French attempts to dislodge the British and Spanish from their positions were resisted until mounting exhaustion and casualties on the French side forced them to retire. As a result of a failure of supplies, the equally exhausted Allies were unable to pursue the retreating French and, eventually, the British returned across the Portuguese border. One of the lessons Wellesley (who, a few weeks after the battle, received his new title of Viscount Wellington) had learnt was that cooperation with the Spanish was, at best, fraught since he was unable to rely on them for supplies and needed to keep in close touch with the supply line provided by the British navy and the wagon train system he was in the process of establishing. Although this restricted what he was able to attempt, it was clearly an imperative for the future.

Soult's failure to hold on to Portugal led to the appointment of the highly experienced Marshal André Massena to achieve the re-occupation of that country. Increasing the number of troops in the Peninsula by over 100,000 men, the emperor gave Massena command of 138,000 men to achieve his objective. Massena moved swiftly to the offensive and set his army in train for the Portuguese border. Wellington determined to inflict an early lesson on the new French commander and prepared a surprise for him at Bussaco ridge – which has been described as one of the best defensive positions in the Peninsula. The ridge was steep and difficult. So steep, in fact, that Massena was unable to bring any of his artillery to bear and so difficult that cavalry could not be deployed on its slopes. Brigade after brigade of the French army struggled up the slopes only to be thrown back by Allied counter-attacks until, eventually, the assault was abandoned with substantial loss.

Eventually, Massena's cavalry found a route which bypassed the ridge and allowed him to enter Portugal. What he found when he arrived at the approaches to Lisbon was a land laid bare by the Portuguese peasantry and a strong series of forts and prepared defences in place, which rendered his huge army virtually impotent. With restricted rations and scant protection from the heavy rains to which Portugal is subject during the early autumn, the French approached the lines of Torres Vedras. To Wellington's amazement, no attack came. Massena assumed the posture of a besieger and dug in around Sobral for a month. Following this, the French retired for about thirty miles to a position on the line Santarem–Rio Maior. Here, they were protected from an Allied attack but there was little to eat and scant forage for the horses. Only an incomplete adherence by the peasants to Wellington's 'scorched earth' instructions left enough for the French to survive – which they managed to do for an incredible five months. As spring began Massena, followed by Wellington's army, took his starving and numerically reduced army northwards to Celorico and then south-eastwards towards Castelo Branco, by this method avoiding a difficult route over the mountains. After a difference with Marshal Ney, Massena diverted his march eastwards and, following a sharp and costly engagement on the River Coa, retreated to his base at Salamanca.

Both Badajoz and Ciudad Rodrigo, the main Spanish fortresses on the Portuguese border, were in French hands. If Wellington was to move on to the offensive, both of these would need to be taken. There was the further consideration that, if they were besieged, French armies of succour would be dispatched to raise these sieges. And this was, indeed, what happened. At Ciudad Rodrigo, no siege was mounted but the Portuguese fortress of

Almeida on the other side of the border was isolated. At the end of April 1811, Massena was approaching Ciudad Rodrigo with the objective of relieving Almeida. Wellington met and defeated him over three days (3–5 May) at the small village of Fuentes de Oñoro but only after a near disaster when one of his divisions became isolated and surrounded.

Wellington's subordinate, Marshal Beresford, commenced the siege of Badajoz on the last day of the Fuentes de Oñoro battle and immediately learnt that Marshal Soult was making preparations to march to its relief. The Spanish armies of Generals Blake and Castaños were to cooperate with the British general and arrangements were made for the three armies to meet at La Albuera, a small town on the Badajoz road – a position indicated to Beresford by Wellington some time before – in order to thwart the relief effort. So began the events which led to the bloodiest battle of the entire war.

Napoleonic Warfare

That warfare in general, and battle in particular, is horrible, terrifying and traumatic is a truism that no mention of gorgeous uniforms, charismatic and fascinating generals, or the insistence that each army was fighting for its own concept of liberty and freedom can hope to ameliorate. Battle has always consisted of one side delivering a series of shocks to the enemy – particularly an enemy general – that destroys its cohesion and confidence in such a way that, if successful, that side can impose or force its own imperatives on the other.

Although the period 1804 to 1815 is termed the Napoleonic period, after its most dominant personality, in reality there was, militarily, little to distinguish it from much of the preceding century of warfare. One of Marlborough's redcoats or *alte Fritz*'s landseers would have felt very much at home if transported, respectively, 100 or 50 years into the future. However, men had already been born who would see the percussion musket, long-range artillery, crude machine guns and sketchy field works relegate the drums, bugles and flying standards to pretty trappings whilst rendering the actions on a battlefield into those of a charnel house.

The Battle of Albuera 1811

Early nineteenth-century armies were nearly all 'teeth': their fighting strength was made up of battalions of infantry, regiments of cavalry and companies or troops of artillery with, in general, little thought given to providing transport for either supplies or medical equipment. Sir Arthur Wellesley, later to become the 1st Duke of Wellington, had substantial experience of setting up a transport system from his service in India and almost his first action when he landed in Portugal, in August 1808, was to contract with the local mayors to provide drivers and bullock carts. Eventually, this system was to help move his Anglo-Portuguese army across Spain and into France. Payment may have been substantially in arrears and, when it arrived, settled through treasury drafts, but there was an exchange of money involved.

The French army, on the other hand, came from a very different tradition. The revolutionaries decreed that war must pay for war, and requisitioned what they wanted from the local population, often at gunpoint and always without paying. Accompanied, more often than not, by ill treatment of the local population, this stirred up bad feeling and even hatred that helped recruitment both to guerrilla bands and to the ever re-emergent Spanish armies.

As the war progressed, the British government paid for more and more of the Portuguese army's supplies, but the Spanish army relied on the goodwill of their countrymen. However, whilst the patriot forces could not afford to alienate their own population, need frequently drove them to it. When Wellington moved across the Pyrenees into France he was eventually forced to supply his accompanying Spanish units from British stocks.

The basic building blocks of an army – horse, foot and guns – were themselves subdivided. By far the most common troops on any battlefield were the workaday infantry of the line. Expected to form the main battle line, these units tended to be less flamboyant in terms of their uniforms and adornments, but it was on their staying power that a general depended. Their role was to stand in the firing line and defeat their enemy, or to summon up the strength and courage to move into close combat –this despite often being poorly fed, unpaid and with little sleep.

Light infantry – *légère* to the French and *ligero* to the Spanish – were a relatively recent addition to any army's order of battle.

Generals had realized the need for scouts and troops able to screen the main force whilst it moved in difficult country, especially once fighting moved to such localities as the Balkans, against the increasingly moribund Ottoman Empire or into the forests of the New World.

At first, the expedient of using locally raised levies was tried, but their undoubted hunting skills and knowledge of the territory were outweighed by their lack of discipline. Once the Austrians had demonstrated the use and value of the Croats raised from their military borders in what are now Croatia, Serbia and Romania, all armies followed suit. For the British, this meant raising units of Scottish Highlanders, or Rangers in the North American colonies. The French did not have the benefit of such wild country, but did their best with the Ardennes, the Pyrenees and the Jura, whilst the Spanish and Portuguese raised units from their own mountains and uplands.

As a by-product of the establishment of these new troops, army commanders were no longer restricted to seeking out battle in the open, but now had troops who could fight in woods, behind hedges, or in other broken ground. Similarly, having units that could form advance and flank guards meant that they could enter restricted terrain, be warned of threats to their flanks and avoid ambushes.

Cavalry had always enjoyed a plethora of designations – *reiters*, *gens d'armes*, demilances, light horse, dragoons, etc. – but were now largely divided into heavy and light cavalry. The French army had resurrected the cuirass for its heaviest regiments, but only one complete unit ever fought in Spain, and that was exclusively on the east coast. Their cuirasses were of little use against close-range musketry but afforded some protection against sword thrusts and cuts. In contrast, there were large numbers of dragoon regiments available. These no longer used their horses to move around the battlefield to fight dismounted, but they were still equipped with muskets and practised infantry drill, which was sometimes useful when fighting the *guerilleros* or in terrain unsuited to mounted action (as at La Coruña).

British dragoons, by contrast, carried a short carbine and there was little now to show their origin as mounted infantry. To confuse things even more, the old horse regiments that had wreaked such havoc on French squadrons when under Marlborough's command had been redesignated as dragoon guards as a cost-cutting measure but with the honorific of 'guards' as a sop to any wounded pride. Except possibly by themselves, they were never considered as household troops.

Light cavalry – hussars, light dragoons or *chasseurs à cheval* – appeared on army lists at the same time as their infantry counterparts, again as a means to provide far-ranging patrols and guards and to assist in the gathering of intelligence. Originally, these units were not expected to be used on the battlefield, but Frederick the Great insisted that his hussar regiments must be able to earn their pay and trained them to back up his heavy regiments. In the Napoleonic period, this tradition was continued to a certain extent as the French 2ᵉ Hussards would demonstrate at Albuera.

Soult's army included one addition gained from France's eastward expansion, an uhlan or lancer regiment from the Vistular Legion, raised from expatriated Poles. Three partitions had erased Poland from the European map, and some Polish patriots saw the French Revolution and its clarion call of freedom as an opportunity to liberate their own country. Taking service either with the revolutionary army or with one of its satellites, they gained reinforcements from Poles serving with the Austrian, Russian or Prussian armies, or from Poland itself once Napoleon began his campaign there in the winter of 1806/7.

Their cavalry units were almost exclusively equipped with the lance, a weapon that had fallen out of favour in Western Europe in the middle seventeenth century, but which they were to wield with great effect at Albuera. Interestingly, the British were not greatly impressed when they met the lance in the Peninsula; it was their experience at Genappe, during the Hundred Days (the period between Napoleon's return to France from exile on Elba in March 1815 and his second abdication after the defeat at Waterloo in June), that caused the War Office to convert four light cavalry regiments to lancers in 1816.

As a result of the paucity in numbers and quality of mounts, the Portuguese and Spanish cavalry arms were seldom anything more than spectators within their own armies. Regardless of intended (paper) strengths, regiments tended to consist of at most two squadrons and could rarely be trusted to even stand in the battle line if threatened by the enemy. So inconsistent were the Portuguese units that Benjamin D'Urban was to complain that units which had charged home like British cavalry at Salamanca turned tail and withdrew shortly afterwards at Majalahonda.

Artillery was divided into either foot (field) or horse units. Since the seventeenth century, the pieces themselves had been getting lighter, both through advances in the gunsmith's art and the redesigning of the carriages to make the guns themselves more manoeuvrable.

Guns were rated by poundage – 4-pounders, 6-pounders, 8-pounders, etc. The British and Portuguese units were equipped with either 6- or 9-pounders, whilst the French used 4- and 8-pounders. Twelve-pounders had been supplied as corps reserve pieces, but were expensive in terms of the number of horses required to pull them. As a result, French commanders had dropped them from their artillery parks and put them into fixed positions. Each unit, whether British or French, also contained at least one and sometimes two howitzers. Unlike the flat trajectory cannon, these pieces fired their shells high into the air in order to reach behind walls or into cover. The shells were hollow iron projectiles filled with gunpowder and fitted with a goose-quill fuse, itself filled with powder and clipped to a length judged by the responsible officer to be correct for the range at which the shell was required to explode. The fuse was inserted, through a hole in the top of the shell so that it penetrated into the gunpowder filling; it was ignited when fired from the howitzer.

As their name suggests, foot artillery units had gunners who accompanied their equipment at the walk. As they were meant to provide support to infantry units and not move either far or fast, this was acceptable. Horse artillery was of more recent invention, with the first units appearing with either the Russian or the Prussian armies during the Seven Years War. Horse artillery was intended to be fast moving, to accompany advance guards, support cavalry units or provide a quick-reacting reserve formation. All of the members either rode their own horses or could ride on the limbers or wagons.

The limbers and caissons carried about 150 rounds of ammunition for each gun and howitzer, normally enough for a complete day's fighting. Only at Leipzig or Waterloo did any gun ever get close to running out. For cannon, the great preponderance of rounds carried were solid cast iron balls. With a range of about 1,000 yards, these used kinetic energy to inflict casualties, smashing anything in their way. For close-range work, canister was fired; this comprised a sealed tin tube containing twenty-four solid iron balls about the size of a table-tennis ball. The shock of exiting the muzzle of the cannon split the tin apart, turning the gun into something like a huge sawn-off shotgun firing birdshot. This was very much an anti-personnel weapon, intended for use both in defence and attack and its effects could be devastating, particularly when two canisters were fired simultaneously from the same gun (double-shotting).

As has been said, howitzers fired common shell, an explosive round that was used either to set buildings alight or to hit units under cover. The British and their allies the Portuguese had one additional projectile. Spherical case had been invented by Henry Shrapnell of the Royal Artillery. When the shell exploded, instead of several pieces of shell casing coming down on or exploding amongst the target, it was sprayed by twenty-four musket balls that had shared the interior cavity with the gunpowder. This 'secret weapon' was expected to have a significant effect in battle, but a great deal depended on the correct estimating of the range and fuse length. No other country tried to build its own version during the period, but it was eventually adopted widely.

Napoleonic battlefields were relatively restricted in size, unlike the sprawling battlefields of the later nineteenth or the twentieth centuries. Communications were dependent on the speed of a horse or the distance over which a general could make himself heard. Units would deploy where they could see one another, for with the mostly flat trajectory weapons systems in use units had to be able to see their targets in order to fire on them.

Apart from skirmishers or when laying ambushes, no army tried to hide its forces from sight until Wellington himself adopted the defensive tactic of moving his infantry behind the military crest of any suitable high ground available, to avoid fire from massed enemy artillery. He also occasionally instructed his men to lie down in their formations so that they were invisible to the advancing enemy until the last moment, when they rose, cheered and fired off a close-range volley. Both these tactics were employed with some success at Waterloo and Beresford, at Albuera, attempted the former tactic prior to the commencement of the battle to deny Soult knowledge of his strength and dispositions. However, generally, with armies wearing uniforms of every colour in the paint box it would have been difficult to employ concealment as a normal tactic – especially in the attack. Infantry were disposed in formations where the men in each rank had their arms in close proximity to those of their neighbour (shoulder-to-shoulder), and where the chest of the second or third man in each file was close to the backpack of the man in front. To fire their muskets, the rear ranks would lean forward into the gaps between each man in front; it was not unknown for the front ranks to be shot by the man behind or for serious burns to be inflicted.

Cavalrymen also rode knee to knee, but their depth was based on the need for their horses to be able to move. Such close formations were a death trap for their members when they were fired on; artillery was able to carve out whole lines at a time, however, it also meant that the soldiers were under close control from their officers and NCOs.

It might legitimately be asked why the formations were so dense. For infantry, the answer lies in the lack of accuracy of the musket carried by most of the men. Although the maximum range was roughly 300 yards, any hope of an individual ball hitting a target at this range was unlikely. Only by massed firing at a massed target at a shorter range – typically 100 yards or less – could sufficiently damaging casualties be caused. For cavalry, a mass target invited heavy casualties, but only if the sight of such a massed formation of tons of threatening horseflesh failed to break the opposing unit's morale first.

It was for these reasons that drillmasters and generals formed their units in such a fashion. By concentrating their firepower across such a small frontage, infantry units could hit their targets with a series of volleys like hammer-blows. The theory behind this was that, if enough of these shocks were inflicted, the enemy's willingness to continue the fight would be weakened. We have enough eyewitness accounts to appreciate that the British held their fire until their target had got to within 100 yards or closer, fired no more than two or three rounds and then took advantage of the chaos caused to cheer and push forward, so threatening and sometimes actually engaging in close combat with musket butt or bayonet.

In theory, a well-trained infantryman could load and fire his musket three or four times a minute, but this was both tiring and, with the need to tear each cartridge open with the teeth so getting gunpowder in the mouth, thirsty work. As a consequence, officers kept the rate down to about two rounds a minute and expected to see their men begin to employ individual fire very quickly.

Experience of Peninsular battles and folk memories of earlier wars meant that the British were willing to hold their fire almost to the last minute, particularly in defensive mode, if it gave them an advantage. Albuera, however, where the British infantry was initially attacking, was to provide a graphic example of what would happen when an opponent was either unwilling to be panicked, or was unable to remove himself because his own formation stopped him falling back before the threat.

Wellington's army also contained a small number of units equipped with rifles, normally the Baker. Some were deployed with Beresford, but not in sufficient numbers to act as a force multiplier. The advantage of the Baker rifle was that it was accurate to a longer range but it was slower to load. This allowed the British to start causing casualties earlier, but if their opponents could close the gap quickly then the faster firing musket would come into its own.

Before the infantry began their fight, however, the artillery would normally have opened the battle. As a gunner, Napoleon had taught his army the value of concentrated bombardments as a means of preparing the way but, except for a few of the early battles in Spain, French commanders rarely did this, preferring to use their guns as a direct support in their attacks. Partly this was because they rarely had sufficient guns to act as a park or grand battery, but equally because the 12-pounders that were best placed to carry this out required too many of the already scarce horses. When artillery did fire, it contributed its own special psychological threat, with a ground-shaking, massive noise and – sometimes – the sight of the projectile heading directly towards its target, which could not avoid it without leaving its formation – a practice frowned upon by sergeants and the colleague in the rank behind. The sight and sound of an 8 or 9 pound ball of solid iron, travelling at several hundred feet per second, hitting a file of men can safely be left to the imagination.

After a few rounds of artillery and infantry fire, the air would become filled with clouds of gunsmoke that would gradually build up and obscure even quite close objects from sight. Inexperienced troops would then fall prey to waking nightmares. Are the enemy creeping up unseen? What are those barely glimpsed shadows in the fog? Which way am I actually facing: towards my friends or my enemies? Experienced troops would learn to pay attention to the sounds around them to make sense of what was happening, but the obscuring smoke mean that it was difficult to keep track of time and distance. At Waterloo, for instance, many of Wellington's battalions were surprised to see the sun sinking in the west when they began their final advance, having seen it high in the sky when the battle had started.

For cavalry, metaphorical cloaks such as this and a useful hollow between two hills meant that they could hope to catch infantry unawares, preferably on a vulnerable flank, before the foot soldiers could form a protective square. As was to be vividly demonstrated at Albuera, the advantage a horse gave to a man in terms of speed and height could be significant, and the cavalry sabre or lance could inflict frightful injuries. Cavalry was a fragile weapon, however. Once used, it needed to be withdrawn to recover its strength and, perhaps more importantly, whilst it could take ground it could not hold it. If steady infantry showed any evidence of wanting to dispute matters, cavalry would be better advised to withdraw and await events or call up some horse artillery to try and change their minds.

The various arms each had their strengths and weaknesses, and a successful general understood and appreciated what these were. Napoleon had taught his generals the value of combined arms tactics, where horse, foot and guns worked in concert. Wellington and his officers had never had that luxury, partly because horses to carry troopers or pull guns were expensive in terms of shipping space and largely unavailable on campaign. Their tactics were built around superbly trained infantry, with the other two arms as supports. It could be argued that the British took far longer than their enemies and allies to appreciate the finer points of combined arms tactics – certainly they were still learning in North Africa in 1942!

Chapter Two

The Participants
and their Commanders

Not all participants approached warfare in the early nineteenth century with the same tactical doctrines, organizations or weaponry. Their general officers were trained in different ways and came from different backgrounds – some from socially elevated positions, others through the ranks and yet others by purchasing their commissions. These differences gave both advantages and disadvantages to the nations and the generals alike. There follows a brief examination of these aspects of the nations involved and some of the senior officers commanding them.

Spain

The parlous situation of the army in many areas of Spain only gave rise to further chaos, with scores of new regiments being created, to which the male peasantry flocked or were directed in their patriotic thousands with the fervent urging of their village priests. There was a lack in almost every area of military necessity – weapons, uniforms, food, horses and training were all in short supply. There were huge gaps in the experience and knowledge of the officers, both at battalion and field level. Many of the commissioned officers held their positions for social reasons and many of the non-commissioned officers had, until recently, been unpaid for so long that they had maintained themselves by street begging. Had the cadres of the old regular army regiments been brought up to strength with new recruits, some hope of a reasonable order and military capability might have materialized but, except in one or two provinces (e.g. Galicia), the new men were formed into 'Regiments of New Creation'. The cavalry lacked horses, the artillery lacked guns and draught animals, whilst the infantry lacked serviceable muskets until the first supplies began to arrive from Britain. They all needed training and, as a result, were virtually unable to manoeuvre in the field, infantry formation changes being among those manoeuvres they found highly problematic. Hence the unexpected appearance of enemy cavalry was something to be dreaded. Probably the most ruinous shortage was that of light infantry. Apart from just 12 battalions (nominally 13,000 men) of light infantry, who were themselves 'light' principally in name only, there was no trained skirmishing force. Each Spanish line infantry battalion included just 32 chosen men who were, theoretically, the best shots and had a capacity for a degree of independence of action. Their main role was to act as the eyes and ears of the battalion on the march. They were also expected to skirmish when the battalion was confronted by enemy light infantry. This was woefully inadequate against the French, who could deploy whole battalions in this role – even line battalions. The shortage was to bedevil Spanish field actions for several years.

In 1801, Spain had fought Portugal in the 'War of the Oranges' and her armies had clashed with those of Revolutionary France in the north-east some years before. These conflicts had generally met with some success and, although the former was not a particularly trying episode, the latter had made something of a reputation for General Gregorio de la Cuesta who had managed to capture the area of France in the Pyrenees known as the Cerdagne – at one time part of the thirteenth-century kingdom of Mallorca. Additionally, the Spanish navy had been in almost continuous contention with that of Britain for many years. There was, therefore, a level of combat experience in the 'old' regular Spanish armed forces despite the limitations the neglect of recent years had engendered.

The Spanish army of 1808 comprised a total of two guard (one

Spanish, one Walloon) and fifty-seven regular army infantry regiments of whom twelve, as has already been said, were light, six were Swiss mercenaries (of long standing), three were originally formed from Irish immigrants and one was nominally Neapolitan. Each guard regiment contained three battalions as did each line regiment except the Swiss, who had two. Light regiments contained a single battalion. During the early years of the war, hundreds of new regiments were raised but little training was possible and units were often rushed into active service within days of their formation. Many battalions were consequently almost impossible for their officers to manoeuvre in battle although the men gradually became as steady under fire as those of any other European nation.

Because of the War of the Oranges several Spanish regiments were stationed in Portugal; thanks to Napoleon's clever strategy, La Romana's division, containing what was probably the cream of the army, was in Denmark, and the rest were spread across Spain. This was not conducive to the establishment of a field army under a single commander and a consequent coordination of objective and effort.

Table 1. The 1808 distribution of Spanish battalions

Guard Infantry

regiment	men	location
Guardias de España	3294	1st & 2nd Bns Barcelona 3rd Bn N.Cast.
Guardias Valonas	2583	1st Bn Madrid, 2nd Bn Barcelona, 3rd Bn Port.

Line Infantry

Brig.	regt. no.	regt name	men	location
1	1	del Rey	1353	1st Bn S.Seb., 2nd Bn Port., 3rd Bn Gal.
	2	de la Reina	1530	Andalucia (3 Bns)
	3	del Principe	1267	Galicia (3 Bns)
	8	de Soria	1311	Balearics (3 Bns)
	27	de la Princesa	1969	Denmark (3 Bns)

The Battle of Albuera 1811

Brig.	regt. no.	regt name	men	location
2	4	de Saboya	936	Valencia (3 Bns)
	5	de la Corona	902	Andalucia (3 Bns)
	6	de Africa	898	1st & 3rd Bns And., 2nd Bn S.Seb
	7	de Zamora	2096	Denmark (3 Bns)
	11	de Sevilla	1168	Galicia (3 Bns)
3	12	de Granada	1113	Balearics (3 Bns)
	13	de Valencia	923	Murcia (3 Bns)
	16	de Toledo	1058	1st & 2nd Bns Gal., 3rd Bn Port
	19	de Murcia	1762	1st & 2nd Bns Port., 3rd Bn And.
	21	de Cantabria	1024	Ceuta (3 Bns)
4	9	de Cordoba	793	Andalucia (3 Bns)
	10	de Guadalajara	2069	Denmark (3 Bns)
	17	de Mallorca	1749	1st & 2nd Bns Port., 3rd Bn Est.
	20	de León	1195	Galicia (3 Bns)
	25	de Aragon	1294	Galicia (3 Bns)
5	14	de Zaragoza	1561	1st & 2nd Bns Port., 3rd Bn And.
	15	de España	1039	Ceuta (3 Bns)
	18	de Burgos	1264	Andalucia (3 Bns)
	22	de Asturias	2103	Denmark (3 Bns)
	23	de Fijo de Ceuta	1235	Ceuta (3 Bns)
6	24	de Navarra	822	Galicia (3 Bns)
	26	de América	808	1st Bn N.Cast., 2nd & 3rd Bns Val.
	29	de Málaga	854	Andalucia (3 Bns)
	30	de Jaén	1755	1st & 2nd Bns And. 3rd Bn Ceuta
	31	de la Ordenes Militares	708	1st Bn Est., 2nd & 3rd Bns And.
7	28	de Estremadura	770	Catalonia (3 Bns)

Brig.	regt. no.	regt name	men	location
	32	de Voluntarios de Castilla	1487	Murcia (3 Bns)
	33	de Voluntarios del Estado	742	Madrid (3 Bns)
	34	de Voluntarios de la Corona	1296	1st Bn Portugal 2nd & 3rd Bns Gal.
	35	de la Infanta de Borbón	1544	Balearics (3 Bns)
8	36	de Irlanda	513	1st Bn Est., 2nd & 3rd Bns And.
	37	de Hibernia	852	1st Bn Asturias, 2nd & 3rd Bns Gal.
	38	de Ultonia	351	Gerona (3 Bns)
	39	de la Infanta de Nápoles	288	Galicia (3 Bns)

Swiss Infantry

	no.title	men	location
1	de Wimpffen	2079	Catalonia (2 Bns)
2	de T Reding (vice Rutiman)	1573	N.Cast. (2 Bns)
3	de N Reding	1809	Andalucia (2 Bns)
4	de Beschard	2051	Balearics (2 Bns)
5	de Traxler	1757	Murcia (2 Bns)
6	de Preux	1708	Madrid (2 Bns)

Light Infantry

regt name	men	location
1st Rto de Aragón	1305	Madrid (½ Bn); Zaragoza (½ Bn)
2nd Rto de Aragón	1225	Balearics (1 Bn]
Cazadroes de Barbastro	1061	Port. (½ Bn); And. (½ Bn)
1st Rto de Cataluña	1164	Denmark (1 Bn)
1st Rto de Cataluña	685	Galicia (1 Bn)
Rto de Taragona	1142	Pamplona (½ Bn); Est. (½ Bn)
Rto de Gerona	1149	Portugal (½ Bn); And. (½ Bn)

regt name	men	location
1st Rto de Barcelona	1266	Denmark (1 Bn)
2nd Rto de Barcelona	1300	Balearics (1 Bn)
Vol. de Valencia	1242	Port. (½ Bn); And. (½ Bn)
Vol. de Campo Mayor	1153	Port. (½ Bn); And. (½ Bn)
Vol. de Navarra	963	Port. (½ Bn); Gal. (½ Bn)

And. = Andalucia; Est. = Estremadura; Gal. = Galicia; N.Cast .= New Castile; Port. = Portugal; S.Seb. = San Sebastian; Val. = Valencia; Ceuta is in North Africa, opposite Gibraltar.

The 'Irish' and 'Neapolitan' regiments contained mostly pure-bred Spaniards but the former retained uniform distinctions from the rest of the army – as did the Swiss – in the colour of their coats. Most of the line regiments at the time of the commencement of the Peninsular War had white coats, the light infantry, guards and Swiss wore dark blue and the Irish a lighter blue. With various regulations having been changed and only partially implemented, however, it is doubtful that this was universal. As the war progressed, supply problems dictated that the average soldier obtained what he could where he could. Enemy equipment was taken from battlefields and intercepted supply columns. The British supplied Spain with a variety of their uniforms, in various colours, and locally produced brown colours were adopted as necessary. Much the same constraints applied to the other arms and the term 'uniform' was largely a misnomer until the issue of a new, two-tone blue national infantry uniform was undertaken in late 1811 – after the battle of Albuera had been fought.

By the time of Albuera, Spain had been at war with France for around three years. As we have indicated, there had been one or two successes in the field – Bailén being perhaps the most significant and complete, since an entire French corps had surrendered – but generally the story was one of consistent and frequently humiliating defeat. Such defeats were by no means entirely the fault of the private Spanish soldier, who (with some notable mounted exceptions) proved himself as brave and steadfast as his foreign counterpart on many occasions. There is no single feature which produced the defeats. A combination of lack of experience and training (from the general officers to the rank and file), paucity of materiel and decent horses, scarce and unreliable avail-ability of food and clothing, lack of central control, and a general and understandable fragility amongst the newest regiments were all to blame. Nonetheless, prior to Albuera, the Spanish, by their own efforts, had beaten the French at Tamames and Alcañiz in pitched battles, resisted their attempts in sieges at Zaragoza (first siege) and Valencia and met with minor successes in raids on the east coast and in northern León.

The remarkable thing about Spanish armies during the war was their incredible ability to survive defeat and rout and, within days, rally, reassemble and be willing to take the field again. Many of the units within a defeated army might be scattered to the four winds after a defeat but, if they could not make their way back to their parent formation, those officers present would frequently obtain local recruits, reform their battalion or regiment and make their way to the nearest Spanish force. In this way, many regi-ments, each with the same or a similar name were represented simultaneously and for varying periods of time, by two or even more different formations. This is why it is so difficult for histo-rians to produce an authoritative list of regiments for the Spanish army of this period.

This resilience, together with the existence of innumerable guer-rilla bands – many of whom behaved like and even became regular units – fed Napoleon's view of the War of Independence as 'the Spanish ulcer'. It continually bled France of men and resources.

Naturally, as the war progressed, men and generals became better at what they did and by the time the Allies pushed the French back across the Pyrenees in 1814 many Spanish formations were a match for whoever came against them. Wellington was appointed Generalissimo of the Spanish army in 1812 and was able to institute some reforms and appoint the more able generals (many of whom had been guerrilla leaders) to positions of respon-sibility. If only the Spanish governing junta had been willing to appoint a single overall commander earlier – General Castaños, who was in overall command in the Bailén campaign was an obvious if not the best candidate – the army might well have fared better, but petty jealousies and rivalry conspired to prevent this.

By the time of Albuera, the process of improvement was making progress but there was still a long way to go. There were signs that more general officers could be relied upon to make proper use of the formations under their command, whilst training and organization were improving all the time. Weaponry (much of it British) was generally of reliable quality and morale was gradually stiffening – even amongst the cavalry. The benefits of these improvements were, perhaps, best seen in the division commanded at Albuera by José Zayas, who had formed his division from troops under his command on the Isla de León, Cádiz, in the latter part of 1810. They had been reorganized into the new six-company battalion formation, with two of these companies designated as grenadier and light respectively. There followed six months of intensive training in the Campo de San José, near Cádiz, using a system of instruction designed by Zayas.[1] As a result of this training, the battalions in Zayas's division were familiar with and practised in established light infantry skirmishing tactics and had achieved a proper level of manoeuvrability in the field. This was to prove decisive at Albuera. It is also entirely likely, although we have been unable to obtain any direct evidence, that they were clothed and armed in a relatively uniform manner – brown and blue being the predominant tunic colours.

The divisions of Zayas and Lardizabal had both taken part in a campaign to raise the siege of Cádiz in February and March 1811, which culminated in the successful Battle of Barossa (or Chiclana, as the Spanish more correctly call it). Unfortunately, the Spanish overall commander, Manuel La Peña, had not cooperated fully with Sir Thomas Graham in charge of the British contingent, and the latter was forced to fight the main action outnumbered and unsupported. Zayas had marched out of Cádiz to join up with La Peña's expedition and, whilst the Chiclana fight was going on, consistently urged La Peña to join Graham's men – but to no avail. He had just successfully linked with Lardizabal to clear Villatte's French division from the siege lines and would have certainly effected a reduction in the heavy casualties suffered by Graham's command in his superb victory. There is a distinct possibility that Lardizabal's men had also benefited from the training regime introduced by Zayas, since they had performed creditably prior to the arrival of Zayas's division.

This, then, was the general state of the Spanish army in the years and months leading up to the Battle of Albuera.

Spanish general officers have generally fared badly at the hands of British historians – as have their armies and, whilst a proportion of the criticism is deserved, by no means do they merit all of it. One must remember that they were products of their environment and the Bourbon monarchy had not treated the military as a major priority in the period prior to the war; indeed, even the attempted reforms of Godoy had not been implemented. By and large, Spanish generals were personally courageous and frequently led armies of mostly untrained, ill-equipped and certainly inexperienced troops. This cannot have made their lives easy and they were occasionally forced to give battle as a result of the patriotic enthusiasm of their men and their political masters – not to mention local pastors of the Catholic church. Several of them, at various times in their careers, presided over victories and effective campaigns. The victorious Reding at Bailén, del Parque at Tamames and Blake at Alcañiz are as deserving of praise as La Peña at Tudela, Venegas at Uclés or Areizaga at Ocaña[2] are of the criticism levelled at them.

The following profiles are provided to assist in illustrating how the backgrounds and experiences of the Spanish general officers who played significant parts in the Battle of Albuera, may have affected their actions and decisions on the day.

Teniente-General Francisco Xavier de Castaños y Aragorri

One of Spain's most prestigious generals, Francisco Castaños was born in Madrid in 1758. His father had gained acceptance at the court of King Felipe V, became ambassador to Parma, army minister and an adviser to the king. When he was just 10 years old, King Carlos appointed Castaños to the rank of infantry captain and he was enrolled in the Seminario des Nobles for the best education he could have received. When he was 16, his father died and he decided on a military career, enlisting in the

Regimiento de Saboya at Cádiz. In the ensuing years, he took part in a number of military activities including the blockade of Gibraltar and, afterwards, the acquisition of Menorca; the Sieges of Orán and Ceuta in Africa followed and, in 1782, he was involved in a combat to support some Spanish and French squadrons. Promotion to colonel of the Regimiento de Africa ensued, in which position Castaños and his regiment participated in the War of the Rosellón. In 1793 he was severely wounded in the defence of San Marcial against the French revolutionary army.

It was in 1804 that Castaños became a lieutenant general, having been promoted to brigadier after San Marcial, and a little later was promoted *mariscal de campo* (equivalent rank to a British major general – *not* a field marshal). When the French invasion came, it was a considerable surprise to Castaños who was in Cádiz and, with uncharacteristic but commendable despatch, assembled a mixed force of six thousand men and advanced to Ronda. He was prepared, with this small force, to face General Dupont, who had already secured the Despeñaperros pass. Castaños's body of troops were considerably reinforced while Dupont was taking Córdoba and the two armies met at Andujar, where the French halted their advance. Something of a stand-off resulted as Dupont awaited the arrival of his colleague Vedel. The two French commanders did not manage their co-operation well and became separated. The Spanish army was divided into several parts, two of which combined at Bailén and were waiting for Dupont as he retired from Andujar. Dupont was comprehensively defeated in the ensuing battle, with Castaños marching against his rear as the battle raged.

Castaños was revered as the 'Victor of Bailén' for the rest of his long life and the church in the town contains his remains, whilst a beautiful memorial now commemorates the battle. Although Castaños was in overall command of the Army of Andalucía at the time of Bailén, it was really Teodoro Reding, the Swiss mercenary, in command of the troops which fought the battle, who achieved the victory. It is not our intention to go into details of that battle now but the plan which led to the battle was the result of a council of war and represented a very dangerous under-taking, requiring the coordination of two or three corps. If

Dupont, commanding the French, had shown more decisiveness and energy, his poorer quality French force might well have defeated the Spanish in detail. His colleague General Vedel could have contributed to this with a little more of the same qualities. Reding certainly took his opportunity and was well-supported by his subordinates in the battle itself. However, Castaños was the commander-in-chief and rightly attracted the plaudits he received. At this point, he was seriously considered as the 'Generalissimo' for the Spanish military. Sadly, the various *juntas* controlling this part of Spain's destiny could not reach agreement and so the opportunity to adopt a unified command for Spain's army was missed. Whether Castaños would have been up to the job militarily is uncertain. He was not the most adept of generals although his education and training were sound in this respect. He was, however, a tactful man – as his efforts to see Beresford take overall command of the Allied troops at Albuera demonstrated – with an appreciation of the wider implications of the cooperation required between Spain and her allies.

Castaños's weakness was on the battlefield. He was dilatory in pursuing Dupont from Andujar to Bailén – his first battle – after discovering the French army had gone from its encampment. In a later battle, at Tudela, shortly after the main Spanish armies had been ineffectually cooperating to attack King Joseph Bonaparte across the Ebro river, the position he decided to occupy was too long and he depended on other Spanish generals both under his direct command and independent of him to supply troops for its occupation. He was ill-served by almost all of them and would have been better advised to seek battle in a more manageable position. The reinforcing troops were late in arriving and many were still crossing the Ebro when the French attack commenced. Castaños had almost 4,000 cavalry but did not deploy them to watch the French and counter the manoeuvres of the enemy horsemen. This was to be a fatal error. The independent force under La Peña did not stir from its position at Cascante, on the far right of the Spanish line (in which there was a huge gap as a consequence) and the predictable disaster followed. As a result of this, Castaños resigned his position; it is to his credit that he had no pretensions of being a great general or overconfidence in his own military capabilities.

The Battle of Albuera 1811

TENIENTE-GENERAL JOACHIN BLAKE

Blake came from emigré Irish stock and was born at Malaga on 19 August 1759. At the age of 15, he was a cadet in the Regimiento de América, later becoming *sergento-mayor* in the Regimiento Voluntarios de Castilla. In 1794, he was wounded at Muga in the conflict against Revolutionary France. A year later, he was appointed *coronel* of the Regimiento Voluntarios de la Corona. When the War of Independence broke out, in 1808, the Galician *junta* appointed him to the rank of lieutenant general and made him captain-general of their province. He showed good military sense early in this position by securing agreement from the *junta* that most of the new recruits joining the Galician army should be used to fill out the ranks of the under-strength regular units of his command. By doing this, Blake ensured that the levies absorbed the experiences of their established comrades and drew confidence from being deployed with them in battle.

His career was to prove one of much ill-fortune with occasional success. He was a fiercely brave and resolute general without the dilatory nature of many of his contemporaries. Although he is described by Oman[3] as having 'neither the slackness nor the arrogance which were the besetting sins of so many of the Peninsular generals', there are instances when the latter defect was in evidence, albeit to a lesser degree.

His first battle – that of Medina de Rioseco – was fought with many of his battalions detached in the mountains behind him on the orders of the *junta* and virtually no cavalry to gather intelligence. His cooperation with Cuesta was not carried out with the two generals on the best of terms and culminated in their two bodies of troops being separated by a considerable distance when the battle commenced, so that mutual support was denied them. The ground chosen by Blake to camp for the night was good but really required greater numbers to occupy it properly when the battle commenced unexpectedly the following morning. His lack of cavalry meant his force was outflanked and scattered by a large body of French horse. Nevertheless, his troops fought well and his handling of the battle was by no means inept; the rout of his army was largely caused by factors outside his control.

His next major conflict, after a number of setbacks (for

example at Zornoza), was to occur at Espinosa de los Monteros as part of the massive Spanish effort to eject Joseph Bonaparte in which Sir John Moore was to have taken part. As a result of the inability of the Central Junta to coordinate Spanish military affairs, Blake's army was, like that of Castaños at Tudela, again scattered, being crushed by better coordinated French action and the absence of the support he expected. Again, there was no lack of courage displayed either by Blake or his troops; they were simply outclassed and outnumbered. He was, shortly afterwards, replaced by La Romana who had returned from Denmark following his escape with the assistance of Britain.

In May 1809, Blake was given the command of the armies of Aragon, Valencia and Catalonia as the 'Army of the Right'. He gathered the forces at his disposal and determined to reverse his fortunes. French forces were being driven back from Aragon by insurgent forces and a large body under Blake's command seized the town of Alcañiz. About 9,000 Spanish then proceeded to hold the town against a concerted French attack with similar numbers. Blake had achieved his aim and regained his self-esteem. However, this was not to remain the case for long. Emboldened by his success, Blake decided to threaten Zaragoza and a battle ensued near the village of Maria. A significant part of Blake's army was isolated on the wrong side of a river and – inexplicably – Blake did not instruct it to join him. As a result an opportunity to inflict a second defeat on Suchet was lost and the French general succeeded in summoning his own reinforcements, completely turning the tables on Blake.

Subsequent operations by Blake in the east were all thwarted in their overall design by the fact that the *juntas* of the three provinces and the local militia leaders would not allow their troops to stray far from home so that Blake was unable to concentrate sufficient men to mount an effective campaign in any particular place. Nevertheless, he was a constant thorn in the sides of the French commanders against whom he manoeuvred. He almost succeeded in his first attempt to raise the siege of Gerona. As a result of the difficulties he had to contend with, Blake, blamed for the ultimate fall of the fortress, quarrelled with the authorities and resigned his position as captain-general.

At the end of January 1810, The Central Junta abdicated after a revolution in Seville and set up a temporary three-man Regency (which included Castaños) to take over the governance of the country. Eventually, after a meeting of the Cortes a proper Regency was established and Blake, who had been called to Cádiz to command the troops there, was made one of the three new regents. In April of the following year, Blake took the two divisions of Zayas and Lardizabal to join Ballesteros in the Allied effort to take Badajoz.

Following Albuera, Blake joined the pursuit of Soult and, at Wellington's request moved on Seville. In July, Blake, after some ineffective and surprisingly timid operations, returned to Cádiz with Zayas and Lardizabal, where he received permission from the Regency to go to Murcia – of which province he was duly made captain-general. Collecting the forces of that province and joining them to his own troops, he set off towards Valencia. For the next six months some fairly lacklustre performances by Blake – who seemed to have lost his spirit – culminated in his capture, following a badly handled battle at Saguntum, at the siege of Valencia. This also saw the divisional generals Zayas and Lardizabal captured and the three were imprisoned at La Vincennes. Blake survived his captivity for many years in France after the fall of Valencia. Released from his detention at Samur in 1814, he died in Spain, at Valladolid, on 27 April 1827.

MARISCAL DE CAMPO JOSÉ LARDIZABAL

We could find no biography of Lardizabal and so will have to limit ourselves to details of his military career. The first time Lardizabal comes to the attention of readers of Professor Oman's great work is as part of the expedition which set out from Cádiz in February 1811. This landed at Tarifa and threatened Marshal Victor's siege of Cádiz by menacing his rear and causing him to move away from his siege lines. Lardizabal had been some time on the Isla de León, and had been given the command of a new Vanguard Division, whose battalions had been assembled together for the first time for this expedition,[4] so it is entirely likely that this was the first active command for him. He was present during the period that José Zayas wrote and implemented his new manual of instruction and, almost certainly, his troops would have had the benefit of training under it.

Lardizabal's men led the column which set out from Tarifa to march along the coast towards Victor. The commander of the expedition, a Spanish general of little skill and a reputation for failing to support his colleagues, Manuel La Peña, squandered several opportunities to cause Victor serious problems and so there was little more than night marches through difficult, often flooded country to occupy Lardizabal. At a place called Casas Viejas, a French outpost was caught in place but it was dealt with by some KGL cavalry under General Graham whose British force was part of the expedition. General José Zayas, remaining in command of the Isla de León garrison, was to lay a bridge of boats across the creek separating the island from the mainland and attack Victor's men in the rear, but the French marshal had laid a trap in the wooded high ground around Chiclana.

After a night march, La Peña's force arrived at Victor's front line, where Vilatte's division was posted and Lardizabal was instructed to mount an immediate attack, despite the fact that his troops had been under arms for some fourteen hours and were exceedingly tired. The five battalions in Lardizabal's division did not have a numerical advantage and their fatigued state meant the initial attack did not succeed. La Peña sent in some reinforcements and the Spanish began to make a little progress when the sounds of musketry could be heard from Vilatte's rear. It was Zayas and his division crossing the creek and attacking the French rear. Vilatte retired and La Peña lost yet another opportunity by refusing to allow Lardizabal to press his attack.

The final outcome of the expedition was not what had been intended, since La Peña continued to vacillate and left Graham to attack, with his British troops, a numerically stronger French force established on the hill behind Chiclana who were threatening the Allied rear after throwing back the small Spanish contingent left to secure it. Had Graham's men not succeeded in their action, it is doubtful many would have survived. But succeed they did, capturing the first French eagle of the war, and dealing a severe blow to French arms. All this occurred whilst La Peña stood by and watched. Zayas pleaded to be allowed to go to the aid of the

British but permission was refused. Eventually, the Allied troops returned to the Isla de León and the French siege was resumed. None of this ignominious behaviour reflected on Lardizabal's performance. He and his men had behaved creditably in the task they had been set and their courage and resoluteness was not in doubt.

Sadly for Lardizabal, he was captured along with Zayas, in Valencia, when the city surrendered early in 1812[5].

MARISCAL DE CAMPO JOSÉ DE ZAYAS

Probably the best divisional commander in the Spanish army at the time of the Battle of Albuera, José Pascual de Zayas y Chacón had been attracted by a military career from his early youth. He was born in Havana in 1772, where his family had lived since the sixteenth century.[6]

He joined the Rto de Asturias on 15 September 1783 and, four years later, was promoted to second lieutenant. In 1789 he was sent to Orán with his regiment as part of the garrison and when, on 9 October 1790 an earthquake destroyed part of the city, killing several hundred soldiers of his regiment, Zayas was injured but survived. He remained in Orán until the Spanish troops left the city in 1792 following a siege in which Zayas did not participate, having been wounded.

In 1793 he joined the artillery of the Army of Navarre (*Ejército de Navarra*) in the war against Revolutionary France. He took part in a number of battles but was taken prisoner on 23 July. He was released on 28 September 1794 and promoted to lieutenant, continuing at the front until the peace treaty of 1795. In that year he went, for garrison duties and shipboard service, to Vigo with the 2nd battalion of Asturias.

Zayas sailed twice to the Americas and back whilst engaged in his shipboard duties. On his second return, his battalion was, on 26 August 1800, transferred to Ferrol for the defence of the city against a British attack. Zayas distinguished himself and was wounded in the Battle of Brión, where the combat was against superior numbers of British troops who landed from naval vessels. On 22 May 1801 Zayas was promoted to captain of grenadiers in the Asturias regiment, serving in several garrison postings.

Zayas was again promoted to major on 6 April 1804 and transferred to the Rto Órdenes Militares. Napoleon had created the kingdom of Etruria from the spoils of the old dukedom of Tuscany; Etruria had been granted, by the French emperor, to Maria Luisa de Bourbon (daughter of Carlos IV and his wife Maria Luisa de Bourbon-Parma). At the end of 1805 Zayas was appointed as an aide to Lieutenant-General O'Farril, whom he accompanied to Etruria with the Spanish division that was bound for that place. Halfway through 1807, Zayas went to Hamburg with his unit as part of the dispositions for preventing British landings from the North Sea. At the end of that year, he returned to the Peninsula, and on 11 March 1808 was made commander of a battalion of the Princesa regiment of line infantry. This regiment belonged to the Marqués de la Romana's Northern Division, a corps which did outstanding work in Denmark, but Zayas did not go with them.

Being in Madrid he was commissioned by the governing Junta to go to Bayonne to inform King Carlos IV of the situation in Spain, which was that Napoleon, in spite of all the promises and pacts, was imposing a French military regime in Spain – a delicate mission for an officer of his comparatively low rank. There is a suggestion that he may have (not for the last time) been mistaken for the Marques de Zayas. José Zayas was detained as soon as he arrived in France, but he had occasion to speak with Pedro Ceballos, Secretary of State to Fernando VII (at that time) and later to Joseph Bonaparte. Zayas was released on 11 May, and went immediately to Madrid.

At Madrid he was ordered to go to La Coruña to join an embarkation of troops for Buenos Aires. When he arrived at Valladolid he witnessed the popular rising of patriots against the French. General Cuesta kept him there, appointing him his chief of staff, which was a position of enormous importance for an ordinary battalion commander.

On 12 June he took part in the defeat at Cabezón, after which Cuesta's troops retired to Benavente, where he and Zayas tried to form their beaten troops into a new army. On 28 June, Zayas went to the pass of Foncebadón to meet with General Blake, who sent him to La Coruña so that he could explain the situation to the *junta* of the kingdom of Galicia. Zayas's report convinced the *junta* that Blake should join his forces with Cuesta's, but they sent secret instructions to Blake not to collaborate too extensively with Cuesta.

With these forces combined but uncoordinated, they were defeated at Medina de Rioseco (12 July). The Spanish forces retreated to Benavente whilst Cuesta's continued towards León. Cuesta, pursued by the French, implemented Zayas's suggestion of making a flanking manoeuvre by Toro, Zamora and Salamanca, which not only freed them from the French pursuit commanded by Bessières, but also from its rearguard. On 1 August at Salamanca he received news of the victory of Bailén. The same day Cuesta made Zayas a colonel.

After Bailén and the consequent French retreat, there was a confrontation between Cuesta and General Castaños which ended with Cuesta's arrest. Zayas, as his subordinate and close collaborator, was stripped of his post of chief of staff of the so-called Army of Castile. These troops, reduced to the division which Zayas had joined, moved towards Logroño. At Logroño they fought several skirmishes with the French. On 25 October Ney attacked Logroño, which he abandoned the next day. General Castaños considered the troops of the division had not fought as well as they could have, so he ordered their dissolution. Zayas found himself without a position.

On 23 November 1808, Zayas presented himself to General La Peña, the commander of the 4th Division, who accepted him into his division, although it is not known whether he gave him a command. On the same day the Battle of Tudela was fought and lost without La Peña's men participating in the fight, in spite of Castaños' having ordered them to do so.

Castaños' troops retreated, arriving at Borja, soon moving on to Calatayud and from there to Sigüenza. Castaños organized a mobile rearguard to cover their retreat, which Zayas joined as a staff officer. In this role he was present at the rearguard's defeat at Bubierca. Finally, without further misfortunes, Castaños' troops (previously the Army of the Centre) arrived at Cuenca on 12 December. There the Duque del Infantado took command of the force. On 25 December the Spanish forces mounted a small attack against Tarancón, which was successful, forcing the French to back down. Alarmed by this minor defeat, Joseph Bonaparte ordered Victor to crush the Duque del Infantado's Spanish forces, which he achieved at the Battle of Uclés on 13 January 1809.

Zayas participated in the action at Tarancón but was not at Uclés because Cuesta, having been appointed head of the Army of Extremadura, reclaimed him for his army. Zayas took command of the Jaén regiment on 8 January. With these troops he participated in the retaking of the bridge at Almaraz on the Tagus on 29 January.

After this the Spanish forces were attacked by the German division of Victor's corps. Zayas, with his men, covered the retreat after the action at Mesa de Ibor. Cuesta ordered a general withdrawal from Medellín through to Trujillo, closely pursued by the French troops. Cuesta's troops went from Medellín to Villanueva de La Serena. Zayas commanded a force of two battalions of grenadiers, which was considered an elite force at this period, reinforcing Cuesta at Villanueva de La Serena where, after a victorious skirmish, Cuesta decided to fight Victor, resulting in the tremendous defeat of Medellín (28 March). In the battle Zayas's forces acted as a reserve of the Spanish left wing. His intervention, at the moment when the Spanish line yielded, was compromised by members of the Spanish cavalry who had created a bottleneck. Zayas was wounded again in this battle.

The withdrawal, under Zayas's direction, after the defeat saved the Army of Extremadura from complete disaster and it was considered that he had fought well. Consequently, when several officers were rewarded, Zayas was among them. He was promoted to brigadier (brigadier-general) with effect from 8 April 1809, and appointed head of the prestigious Vanguard division of the army.

Zayas's Vanguard organized small attacks against Victor's forces, using 'hit and run' tactics which were very suitable for weakening their enemy. French forces between the Tagus and the Guadiana – all of Victor's corps – could not hold their positions, partly because of the lack of provisions and partly because of Zayas's attacks.

Victor's situation worsened when Soult was defeated in the

north of Portugal. Victor ordered a retreat on the right bank of the Tagus on 14 June. Zayas's troops followed on his heels as far as Almaraz, with the river between them. A few days later, on 6 July, Cuesta and Wellington met at the pass of Miravete. The campaign of Talavera had begun.

During this campaign Zayas's performance was good. His Vanguard was the body chosen to outflank the French and drive them from Talavera on 21 July. During the battle itself the Vanguard division did not see action, since its sector was not attacked and, after the retreat towards Puente del Arzobispo, Zayas's unit covered Cuesta's rear. In the ensuing combat at the bridge of Arzobispo, Zayas's men intervened to stabilize the situation after the French strike, although it did not have occasion to fight, since the French did not exploit their momentary success. Zayas's troops also behaved well in the Battle of Alcabón on 26 July.

These performances did not go without their reward, so on 28 July he was promoted to *mariscal del campo* (major-general). On 12 August Cuesta was attacked at Deleitosa and was replaced in command by General Eguía, who confirmed Zayas in command of the Vanguard.

Immediately afterwards one of the most disastrous decisions of the war was taken. The Central Junta ordered Eguía to unite with the Army of La Mancha (defeated at Almonacíd) for progress towards Madrid. This combined armed force would be commanded by General Areizaga, with Zayas commanding the same Vanguard division.

After crossing La Mancha from south to north Areizaga's troops met the enemy rearguard at Ocaña. On 19 November Marshal Soult attacked the Spanish forces, which he defeated. Zayas's Vanguard acted as a reserve, unleashing a brilliant rearguard action that was able to halt the French, until scattered soldiers from other divisions became entangled among the lines of the Vanguard troops, creating confusion and ruining the Vanguard as an effective force. Zayas's troops still managed to reform at Dos Barrios, 8 km from Ocaña. There they met with the rest of the army and retreated to the Sierra Morena.

On 20 January 1810 Marshal Soult's forces arrived at the pass of Despeñaperros, defeated the defenders and penetrated into

Andalusia. Zayas's forces (the survivors of Ocaña) retreated to Úbeda and Jaén. Little by little the retreat wore away its units to the extent that, at the later actions of Jaén and Alcala Real, its participation was virtually symbolic.

After the Andalusian defeat Zayas went to Murcia, where he tried once more to raise soldiers, train them, get them fit and form a new army. However, Zayas stayed only briefly in Murcia since, by 4 March, he was at Cádiz commanding the army division that defended the city against French attack. At Cádiz Zayas wrote a work titled 'Instructions on Good Military Order',[7] a real manual on how to organize troops on campaign. Under his leadership this unit became one of the best divisions of the Spanish army. Zayas's troops harassed the French episodically with their 'hit and run' tactics, similar to those already used in Extremadura.

On 21 February 1811 the forces defending Cádiz began a flanking manoeuvre with which they hoped to defeat the besiegers (commanded by Marshal Victor). The Spanish forces disembarked between 23 and 27 February at Algeciras and Tarifa, with instructions to follow in Victor's rear as far as Medina Sidonia, and after defeating him (which should not be difficult), to follow him towards Cádiz to complete the lifting of the encirclement. Meanwhile Zayas, at the head of the troops on the Isle of León, would cross the channel that separates the island from the mainland to attack Victor's forces. Zayas carried out his part of the plan on the night of 2/3 March, but on the 3rd, due to the failure by La Peña to keep to the agreed timetable, was beaten while crossing the channel and was forced to fall back to his starting point. The disembarked troops had been delayed as a result of La Peña's irresolution, so the combined manoeuvre was a debacle. Zayas's promotion to *teniente general* was rescinded and was not reinstated until 1814 – rather a harsh reaction to a single misfortune in what had been a faultless performance until then.

Soon after this, Zayas was placed at the head of another flanking operation. On 18 March he left Cádiz by boat with his forces to disembark at Palos. The idea was to follow the Seville highway, threatening the flank of the forces under Soult which were besieging Badajoz. However, the frontier city had surrendered on 11 March and Soult could confront the threat. On 31

March, after several battles with the French vanguards, and seeing how bad their situation was, Zayas's troops returned to Cádiz.

Shortly after this plans were made to retake Badajoz by means of a combined attack by General Beresford's Army Corps, plus a force, called the Expeditionary Corps, under General Blake. Zayas commanded the 4th Division of this corps.

The Expeditionary Corps disembarked at Ayamonte on 18 April to go up along the course of the Guadiana to meet with the British and they duly met at Albuera on 15 May. On 14 June Zayas's troops assaulted the Niebla castle, but the attack failed because of a shortage of artillery. Shortly after this Blake received information that Marmont's forces had united with Soult's and were advancing on him. Blake prudently ordered a retreat. On 30 June Zayas's forces embarked at Ayamonte for a return to Cádiz.

At the beginning of August the Expeditionary Corps was sent to Valencia as part of the effort to prevent Suchet from conquering Valencia and Murcia. On 14 August Zayas accompanied Blake to Valencia. His division was at Villena until 21 September, in quarantine because of an epidemic (and therefore useless for combat). Zayas's division was then sent to Valencia to garrison the entrenched camp that defended the city. On 25 October Zayas's troops left Valencia. Blake, pressured by local politicians, was looking for battle. Zayas's division attacked Puzol and continued northwards, arriving in sight of Sagunto, which was surrounded by the French. Nevertheless, the rest of Blake's forces had been defeated and Zayas had to retreat before the enemy. A battalion of his division was surrounded at Puzol and destroyed. The rest of the division, in good order, withdrew by the coast, constantly fighting rearguard actions. The retreat allowed the centre and left wings of Blake's army to be saved.

After this combat Zayas marched with his troops to Cuenca to block the shipment of reinforcements to Suchet from Madrid. In the middle of December Zayas returned to Valencia. It was just in time since on 26 December Suchet mounted his attack against Blake. Zayas's troops fought well, but Blake's forces were surrounded and were ordered to retreat inside Valencia, which was then surrounded by the enemy.

The French repulsed an attempt to break out on 28 December.

At the beginning of January they began to bombard the city. With little food, almost without ammunition and with a very high desertion rate (except in Zayas's unit), Valencia surrendered on 10 January 1812. Zayas was captured by the French and was sent to the castle of Vincennes, which had been turned into a jail for the nobility and members of the Spanish high command who had been taken prisoner.

At the beginning of 1814 the French, who confused him with the Marqués de Zayas, decided to send him to Madrid to try to get the Regency to accept the Treaty of Valençay, signed on 11 December 1813 by Fernando VII and Napoleon. In spite of this mix-up Zayas travelled to Madrid with the Duque de San Carlos, who actually carried out the mission.

From this moment Zayas was left without a post, despite being available and of proven ability. On 25 March 1814 he was at last promoted to lieutenant general. During the Hundred Days Zayas commanded the 1st division of the Army of the Right, entering France via Cataluña. There was hardly any action since Napoleon's forces were concentrated in the north. After Napoleon's second abdication Zayas left, bound for Valencia.

He did not return to the command of troops. He retired from the service and died in 1827, although there is doubt as to whether he was in Madrid or in his native Havana. Zayas's career had been virtually spotless and replete with well-organized and highly effective actions. It is interesting to wonder what an independent field command would have produced from him.

TENIENTE-GENERAL FRANCISCO LÓPEZ BALLESTEROS
Ballesteros was a highly politically motivated officer and constantly tended to promote his own interests over those of the national cause. This led to a temporary downfall from favour and incarceration. However, he was popular with his compatriots and the populace at large.

Although a relatively young man, Ballesteros had retired from the military, where he had been an officer in the infantry. In 1808 he was working in the tobacco industry – which was effectively state-owned – when he was appointed to the Asturian army and promoted to *mariscal de campo* by the regional *junta*. There was a substantial French presence and base of operations at the port of Santander, against which Ballesteros mounted a highly successful raid. Probably resulting from this success, he was placed in charge of a division of Asturian troops and advanced into León as reinforcement for the Army of the Left (*Ejercito de la Izquierda*). However, his division did not accompany that body when it went to the Badajoz area, instead being ordered to operate on the Andalucian borders in much the same role he had adopted in the Santander operations. From February 1810 onwards, this was the operation Ballesteros had been conducting with some effect when he was posted to join Beresford's army for Albuera.

The troops under Ballesteros's command were known for being undisciplined and he had received criticism from Wellington about this. Rather than modify his approach and the behaviour of his troops, Ballesteros typically adopted an injured dignity stance and persisted in his activities. Supplies for other formations in the Albuera campaign were plundered, as were depots along the Portuguese frontier. This led to a poor relationship with Zayas whom Ballesteros let down very badly.[8] Eventually, the Regency decided enough was enough and, after Albuera, his command was moved to an area near Algeciras.

Despite his ongoing self-publicity as a hero and winner of incredible victories (little of which bore any serious scrutiny), Ballesteros was still a constant thorn in the French side with raids and harassment. His egoism knew few bounds; towards the end of 1811, he sent two of his *aides de camp* to Britain where they were tasked with raising funds to support his division from the British public. The Spanish newspapers were replete with announcements of Ballesteros's exploits (including one that claimed for him the capture of Seville) – few, if any, of which merited even a column or two.

He strongly opposed the appointment of Wellington as Generalissimo and began to lambast the Regency for handing the reins of military power to a foreigner. He went as far as to say that he would resign if Wellington was appointed and commenced a vitriolic campaign against the Regency itself. This was the last straw and he was dismissed and placed under arrest preparatory to exile to Ceuta in Africa. Ballesteros was eventually released by the Cortes when the fighting had moved out of Spain and into the Pyrenees.

France

The subject of the French army of the Napoleonic wars is huge and it is not our intention to go into it in great detail here. A fairly full and detailed analysis is given in other works, amongst which is one by the authors of this book.[9] However, it is important to give a picture of France's troops in the Iberian Peninsula between 1808 and 1814 and how they were organized and fought.

During this period, Napoleon Bonaparte had, at various times, up to 300,000 men occupied in subduing the Spanish and Portuguese people, fighting their and the British expeditionary armies and quelling the multitude of guerrilla bands which preyed on French detachments and supply trains. The emperor only ventured into Spain once himself and ensured he had with him the best of his regiments in sufficient numbers for him to be best placed to achieve his goals: the occupation of Madrid, the re-establishment of his brother Joseph as king and the driving of the 'English leopard[10] into the sea'. The first two of these objectives were duly attained but then Sir John Moore enticed a large proportion of Napoleon's army into the remote north-east of Spain and defeated one of his best marshals, before his men embarked on their ships and returned to Britain. This result accomplished the emperor's desire with regard to the 'English leopard' but probably not quite in the manner he had hoped. It also gave the Spanish armies, defeated earlier by Napoleon, time to reform and reorganize. However, before the battle at La Coruña had occurred, the emperor had returned to his homeland to deal with Austria and avoided the embarrassment of commanding a frustrated army hundreds of miles from its proper place.

All this having been said, the French story is one of dogged determination, gritty persistence and near success. The French army in Spain was a mixture of parts of the guard (in small numbers), veteran units from the German campaigns, foreign allies from Germany and Italy and raw recruits. As a result of the way the war was fought, a constant stream of additional men trudged their way across the Pyrenees and joined their comrades in one of the militarily most inhospitable theatres in Europe. Likewise, as the emperor's need for reinforcement in other parts of Europe manifested itself, experienced troops were withdrawn, thus weakening their comrades' position. This, then, was 'the Spanish ulcer' that undermined the French Empire and slowly bled it of its soldiers.

Apart from the one personal involvement by Napoleon described above, the conflict was prosecuted by a number of French marshals. In theory, Joseph Bonaparte and his chief of staff, Marshal Jourdan, were in overall command. In reality, however, the marshals were neither practically required by the emperor to subject themselves to the orders of Joseph or Jourdan nor did they feel so constrained. Indeed, such was the rivalry between these men that the French suffered much the same lack of centralized control as the Spanish – with the same deleterious effects. Continual interference from afar by Napoleon himself added to the confusion, in the form of instructions that were out of date and inappropriate to the circumstances pertaining by the time of their arrival. Demands by one marshal for reinforcements from another's command were ignored or met only in part and there never seemed enough men to carry out all the tasks required of them.

As one province was subdued, insurgency broke out in another. As one Spanish army was defeated, so another reformed and took the field. Despatches were intercepted and supply trains raided by guerrilla bands and laced through it all was the constant and apparently insurmountable threat of the British expeditionary army. Britain retrained the ineffective Portuguese army and it became a major reinforcement to its mentors, increasing and intensifying the pressure brought to bear on the overstretched French. Consequently, French designs were thwarted and their successes nullified. Frustratingly, so much of French intentions and plans seemed to be divined by their enemies that they found it difficult to gain and retain any advantage. This problem was the result of the excellent work done by the British network of intelligence gathering presided over by Major George Scovell, whose unstinting efforts and brilliant mind enabled him to decipher captured French communications so that Wellington could plan his operations with a degree of certainty as to enemy strengths dispositions and even intentions.[11]

The French and their allied nations were organized on the corps basis which had proved so effective in other theatres. A marshal had command of substantial numbers of all arms with which to carry out his orders and they were usually of superior quality to those of their enemy. A French infantry regiment, whether line or light, comprised one depot and four field battalions of which anything from one to four might be present in their division at any one time. Comprised of six companies, including one grenadier and one light, the battalion consisted of around 700 men at full paper strength. Of the cavalry, there was only ever one cuirassier regiment present in the Peninsula – the 13th. Otherwise, divisional support cavalry was made up of hussars or chasseurs for scouting and screening purposes and 'battlefield cavalry' consisted of several mounted dragoon regiments who could fight on foot if the need arose. A cavalry regiment, at full strength, had four squadrons of 150 men each. The artillery was well organized and disciplined and usually outnumbered that of the enemy. The nominal complement of a field artillery company was six cannon (8-pounder or 12-pounder) and two howitzers but this was frequently not achieved for a variety of reasons. Horses were of gradually deteriorating quality over the period of the war, and they were not looked after especially well, particularly by the dragoons, to the extent that British cavalrymen claimed they could smell a French dragoon regiment several miles off because of the horses' saddle sores.

One of Napoleon's innovations was that of the medical corps. Field ambulances accompanied the armies and surgeons were trained to treat battlefield casualties. However, in common with their enemies, the French were not aware of the effect of bacterial contamination, so wounds and disease accounted for numerous deaths – the latter far in excess of the former.

Finally, French engineering was of an excellent quality and each corps included a complement of engineers, sappers and miners.

As well as their German (from Bavaria, the Rhine Confederation, Westphalia, etc.), Italian and Neapolitan allies, the

French army included some Polish (Vistula Legion) regiments and established a number of Spanish units which it recruited from both Spanish (*afrancesado*) and French nationals. Joseph Bonaparte formed a guard from Spanish recruits. Some of these formations would fight at Albuera in 1811.

Whenever the French met the Spanish in battle, they expected to emerge victorious and usually did – with a few notable exceptions. Superiority in cavalry and artillery were the main reasons, coupled with the quality of their generals and troops. The French had been fighting in Europe and elsewhere for the best part of fifteen years by the time the Peninsular War started and they had emerged victorious against such nations as Austria, Russia and Prussia – of no mean military reputation themselves. Self-belief, experience and competence were the key French attributes, coupled with the military genius of the emperor himself. Organizationally, the French had proved themselves superior to any of their enemies and their reputation for speed of strategic movement, tactical awareness and moral strength had made them masters of the European battlefield. The Spanish could boast none of these advantages and had to learn the hard way.

The army corps system gave the French a strategic advantage over those enemies who did not employ it; their staff system was probably the best in Europe and this gave them distinct benefits in manoeuvring to place their opponents at disadvantage. French battlefield tactics were to attack their enemy using 'preparation' by a substantial artillery bombardment before the infantry arrived, although this was not always possible. Infantry formations would advance, following up this bombardment and preceded by a dispersed skirmish line of independently acting light troops. These might be from detached *voltigeur* companies of line and light battalions or might be entire battalions broken into extended order and deployed to screen the advance of their formed, close order comrades behind. The French drill manuals called for the skirmishing light troops to divert to the flanks of the close order formations when these were near enough to launch their attack. The advancing columns of infantry were supposed to deploy into line and give fire to their already demoralized opponents – thinned by artillery and skirmisher fire. Experience had shown them, however, that if the columns showed sufficient aggression and determination, enemy morale would collapse and deployment into line become unnecessary.

Occasionally they would find an enemy who would not give way against this method of attack, in which case the prescribed French tactic would be to halt their columns and deploy the battalions into line, each with three ranks of men, and endeavour to see the foe off with musketry. It was seldom that this proved necessary, except against the British or Portuguese and, in these cases, the French discovered that it was difficult or impossible to perform the manoeuvre since they were themselves under heavy fire.

Whichever nation's infantry achieved supremacy over their enemy, their cavalry would have the task of converting retirement or retreat into full rout by charging the troops falling back. During the preparatory moves of a battle and throughout proceedings thereafter, cavalry would endeavour to place itself on the flanks of enemy formations, from which position a charge could effectively destroy those formations in place. Opposing cavalry would itself manoeuvre to similar purpose and the two sides would try to nullify the effects of each other's horsemen. It was virtually suicidal for cavalry to charge infantry or artillery frontally. French cavalry was, for much of the Napoleonic period, superior to its opponents by some degree. However, in the Peninsula, its dragoon-based formations and lack of good horses cancelled out some of its superiority.

As a consequence of much of the foregoing, French arms were highly successful early in the war but became gradually less and less effective as their enemies gained in numbers, experience and equipment, and they were eventually evicted, first from Portugal and then from Spain.

Marechal 'Nicolas' Jean de Dieu Soult, Duc de Dalmatie

Of the French marshals who served in Spain, Jean de Dieu Soult was undoubtedly one of the best and most consistent. He was respected if not admired by the British private soldier who referred to him as 'Marshal Salt'. Wellington certainly saw him as a dangerous opponent. However, his own men were less enamoured and bestowed on him the nickname 'Nicolas' or 'Old Nick' (which, interestingly, was applied to Napoleon after the Hundred Days). This is a not uncommon nickname and was used for those who were perceived to have committed some serious error or 'crime'; it was certainly uncomplimentary and may have resulted from the allegations that he attempted to form a Portuguese kingdom, with himself wearing the crown. He and Marshal Ney were fierce rivals and Ney's troops referred to Soult as 'King Nicholas'. Born in the same year as both Arthur Wellesley and Napoleon Bonaparte (1769) Soult had aristocratic blood but his own family were artisans – glass makers – and were certainly not wealthy. His Christian name probably reflects the pious Catholic belief of his mother but, in many histories, he is called by his nickname.

Soult was hard to control as a boy and, whilst he was making several abortive attempts to find a career in the area surrounding his family home in the Black Mountains, his mother fell on seriously hard times. The young Soult volunteered for the army, giving his mother the money he obtained thereby and so started on the path that was to produce one of France's most competent soldiers.

In 1785, he joined his first regiment – the Royal Regiment of Infantry – in which he served for two years, achieving the exalted rank of corporal. Since his noble blood was not of a colour sufficiently blue to obtain a commission, disillusionment started to set in: Soult was ambitious and wanted advancement. The frustration that this caused got him into some serious trouble and he was lucky not to be cashiered. He attempted to leave of his own accord and go into the baking business but the attempt was not successful and he had to buckle down in his chosen career. This led to advancement to the rank of sergeant. Eventually, when the year 1792 arrived and with it the invasion of France by Prussia and Austria, Soult had already espoused the Revolutionary cause and was able to take advantage of a unique opportunity that only the Revolution could have brought.

The new volunteer or *fédérés* units elected their officers – all, that is, except for the adjutant. The rank was filled by existing army officers (including non-commissioned men) and it was this position that Soult was to fill in the National Guard (Battaillon de l'Haut Rhin). In this position, it was not long before Soult assumed effective command of the unit; his commanding officer had little experience of command and was elderly. Soult achieved great popularity with his men and with several influential figures in the army. His military exploits showed him to be an excellent leader: brave and resolute, with great initiative and determination. By 1793, Soult's exploits gained him a staff position with one of General Hoche's subordinates and an immediate command that provided an excellent opportunity to shine. In an action close to Niederbronn, Soult's force of infantry, cavalry and artillery attacked the Austrians and comprehensively defeated them. This was followed by a command under General Lefebvre when the division was under severe pressure. Soult dealt with a highly excited and desperate General Marceau and prevented him from showing himself up in Lefebvre's presence. From this point on, Soult enjoyed and deserved rapid promotion; by 1795, he was in command of a demi-brigade.

In 1799, the Second Coalition – a partnership between Russia, Britain and Austria – had declared war on France. Bonaparte was in Egypt and Soult had been mouldering as a chef-de-brigade in the 'Army of England' (a vain attempt by the French Directory to threaten Britain with invasion). The new conflict provided Soult with the perfect opportunity to take a major role. Most of France's best generals were in Egypt and she sought able young commanders to act as replacements. Soult was given command of the advance guard of Jourdan's army (Jourdan was not a competent commander as he was to prove as Joseph Bonaparte's chief of staff in Spain ten years later). The Battle of Stockach was something of a disaster for Jourdan, although not for Soult, who took command of the rearguard division in the well-organized retreat.

This event led directly to the offer to Soult of a division in the Army of Switzerland. Commanded by André Masséna, whom Soult much admired – and with reason – the army was charged with restoring peace to the quarrelling southern Swiss cantons. Soult realized that there was more than a military job to be done. The Helvetic Republic, as Switzerland had come to be known, was of great strategic importance as a barrier between France and

Austria. Both nations were disliked or even hated by the Swiss – whose cantons could not get on with each other. Soult realized that if he could both quell the riotous cantons where several French citizens had been murdered but act in a firm, though restrained manner, he might gain their respect and confidence. He fought a battle with two of the districts and entered into a compact with a third; finally, he visited the shrine to William Tell, committing himself to the charge of Swiss boatmen who could have dealt with him much as their neighbours had dealt with other Frenchmen all too recently. This struck a chord with the Swiss and Soult had achieved his objective. The year was still 1799!

This experience must have contributed considerably to Soult's later activities in the Peninsula when he was frequently called upon to display diplomacy as well as military acumen, which he invariably did with much success. There were other opportunities in Switzerland for Soult to display his talents and he took them all with great relish, receiving the high praise of his hero Masséna in so doing.

The next move for the future marshal was, at the age of 31 and once more with Masséna, to the Army of Italy, in command of the right wing. It was in this post that he suffered his first major setback. Honoré Gazan, one of Soult's divisional commanders (as he was later to be at Albuera in Spain) was commanded to create a diversion during an attack to relieve pressure on the city of Genoa. A terrible storm completely ruined the diversion and Soult's small force was overwhelmed and he was severely wounded and captured. After carrying out an operation on himself to remove the ball from his leg, Soult received attention from Masséna's personal doctor, who had been allowed through the lines for the purpose. Despite these attentions, the wound worsened until Soult was forced to offer his parole. This was accepted and Soult was able to take proper exercise thereby accelerating the healing process.

Although Soult could not take further part in hostilities, he was allowed to utilize his administrative talents and used conciliation to effect a similar result in Piedmont as he had in Switzerland. Prisoner exchange followed soon after and Soult could return to France and resume his military career.

Once Napoleon had become consul, Soult's reputation came to his ears from the likes of Masséna and, in typical fashion, Bonaparte made him colonel-general of the chasseurs of the consular guard. There rapidly followed, in 1803, his appointment as commander of the military camp at St-Omer, from where the intended invasion of Britain was to take place – echoes of the experience in another 'Army of England' four years earlier. Within a year, he had been made a marshal of France.

There followed one of the most successful military careers in the history of the empire. Soult led his 4th Corps de l'Armée to victory at Landsberg, they were involved at both Memmingen and Hollabrünn and then, at Austerlitz in December 1805, the event that made Soult's name something to be conjured with. He had been held in position by the emperor for most of the early part of the battle, fought before dawn. The Russians occupying the Pratzen Plateau had begun to move off to commence a massive attack on the French centre. Napoleon realized this would leave his enemy vulnerable to a counter attack. Soult was asked if he could take the plateau with 4th Corps and his reply was that this could be done in twenty minutes. As the sun rose, Soult moved his troops out, climbed the slope and appeared to the dismay of the Russians almost in their midst. Rapid orders were sent out for troops to retake the position and these men began to climb the slopes. Pratzen village was occupied – and immediately attacked and cleared by Soult's advancing battalions. Marching steadily on at the point of the bayonet, the French sent battalion after battalion of Russians streaming away. Counter attacks were mounted but these were met with resolution and élan by the unstoppable 4th Corps. Within the allotted time, Soult's promise had been fulfilled; it was a brilliant tactical feat. Napoleon had earlier remarked 'one sharp blow and the war is over' and it was Soult who struck that blow.

Awarded the sobriquet 'le premier manoeuvrier d'Europe' by the emperor, for the way he had moved, deployed and controlled his men, it was a glittering moment in Soult's life. There followed, less than a year later, yet another glowing tribute: 'Marshal Soult is the best of all the generals of Europe, the most capable of manoeuvring great masses, of taking the major role on a field of battle, of doing wonders at the head of a French army.' This followed the victory at Jena and the taking of Lübeck in 1806. Then came Bergfried, Eylau, Heilsberg and Königsberg and, in June 1808, after being named Governor of Old Prussia, he was awarded the title Duke of Dalmatia.

There followed what must have been one of the most dogged displays of military persistence in the history of warfare. Soult went to Spain to replace Bessières as commander of 2nd Corps. It surely ranked high amongst Soult's most frustrating experiences. Nevertheless, although ultimately unsuccessful, it included two battles that some historians argue over in terms of who won: Soult or his British adversaries. It also ended with a battle that need never have been fought and that accounted for the deaths of many brave men. The three battles of which we speak are La Coruña in 1809, Albuera in 1811 and Toulouse in 1814.

At La Coruña, Soult had pursued Sir John Moore's disintegrating army for weeks in the bitterly cold, inhospitable mountains of Galicia. Moore was trying to save as much as he could of Britain's only field army. Soult had been charged by the emperor with preventing this or 'throwing the British leopard back into the sea'. It is a moot point whether, by this, Napoleon intended to indicate that he wanted the British army destroyed (which he almost certainly did) or sent packing in their ships away from Spain. At the end of the battle of La Coruña, Soult remained in possession of the field. The British had managed to hold him off long enough for the bulk of their troops to board waiting naval vessels but sail away they did and he had severely mauled them in the process, killing one of their best generals. For the British, they claim it was always Moore's intention that the French should be held whilst successive formations boarded the ships. So one may spend many hours speculating but Soult emerges from the argument as a general of substance. The second battle was Albuera, which reinforced the reputation of Soult's tactical ability but, again, left him without a crowning success.

Finally, after a masterful campaign through the Pyrenees, in which Soult inflicted checks and retreats on his enemies, and then a difficult retreat, once the Allies had invaded France, the two armies fought their last battle roughly a week after Napoleon's signature was applied to the deed of abdication. Toulouse was not quite a siege but Soult's positions in front of the town were behind entrenchments and were supported by guns of position. It was a hard nut to crack and the armies paid a heavy price, Soult losing 3,250 men and Wellington 4,500. Soult realized, towards the end, that he could not prevail and took his army away on the evening of 11 April 1814.

There is a fairly substantial postscript to the story of Marshal Soult, who had joined the revolutionary army as a headstrong and turbulent youth and ended as one of his country's most respected marshals. When the Bourbon king Louis XVIII ascended the French throne, he appointed Soult as his Minister of War. Despite this, and Soult's description of the erstwhile emperor as a 'usurper and adventurer' (perhaps 'opportunist' would be a better translation), on his return, Napoleon felt certain enough of him to reinstate Soult and make him chief of staff for the Hundred Days campaign. The marshal, as ever, discharged his duties with skill and faithfulness but the days of the domination of Europe by Napoleonic France came to an end with the defeat at Mont St Jean. This was not the end, however, of the career of Jean de Dieu Soult. After three years of banishment and disgrace, he returned to the service of King Louis and again became a marshal in 1820. He was the Bourbon's Minister of War from 1830 to 1832, holding several government positions (including Minister for Foreign Affairs) thereafter, attending the coronation of Queen Victoria as the French representative and simultaneously renewing his acquaintance with a certain Arthur Wellesley. The two erstwhile enemies greeted each other with great cordiality and were soon to be seen reminiscing almost like old comrades.

GÉNÉRAL DE DIVISION BARON JEAN BAPTISTE GIRARD

Girard commenced his military career at the age of 18, joining a volunteer battalion in the Barjols district of Provence, close to Aups in the Var district where he was born on 21 February 1775. A year later, he was serving in the Army of Italy under Marshal André Massena. He became an *aide de camp* to General Monnier and then progressed to captain in the 85th infantry regiment. By 1799 he had achieved the rank of *adjutant general chef de brigade* and the following year was chief of staff to Monnier in the Army of Reserve.

1802 saw him in the Italian republic and 1805 on the staff of no less a man than Marshal Murat himself. He served at both Austerlitz and Jena and was promoted *général de brigade* in November 1806. In this capacity, he went to Poland the following year, following which he joined the Army of Spain and commanded the 1st division of Mortier's corps under Soult at the combat of the Arzobispo Bridge, where seventeen guns lost at Talavera were recovered. The Battle of Ocaña, three months later, saw Girard and Zayas engaged in a struggle in which both received high credit for their performances. Saint-Chamans described Girard as 'a young man of great bravery and who had contributed hugely to the winning of the battle of Ocaña'.

Girard served in Spain until 1812 and then took command of a division of IX Corps for the Russian campaign under Marshal Victor. Wounded at Smolensk and at the Beresina crossing, Girard survived the ill-fated Russian adventure and in the 1813 campaign commanded a division in Saxony. He fought at Lützen, where he was again wounded quite severely. Joseph Bonaparte said of him:

> Girard, one of the more brilliant officers of the Imperial Army; this is the same general officer who, hit by three balls at the battle of Lützen, did not want to be taken from the field of battle, saying: 'It is here that whoever has a true French heart must win or die . . .' Napoleon said to his widow at Malmaison: 'if all my generals conducted themselves like the brave Girard, I would not be here'.[12]

Following his recovery, Girard was blockaded in the fortress of Magdebourg and did not return to France until the Restoration. He became a peer of France and was posted to the Army of the North in 1815.

In the Hundred Days, he was engaged in taking the village of Saint-Amand during the battle of Ligny on 16 June, when he received a mortal wound. Girard died in Paris a few days later.

GÉNÉRAL DE DIVISION DEO GRATIAS NICOLAS, BARON GODINOT

Godinot commenced his military career as a cavalryman. At the age of 22, in 1787, he joined the dragoon Régiment de Montmorency but moved to the light infantry and by 1792 was a captain in a chasseur battalion. He was posted to the *Armée de Moselle* and then to the *Armée de Sambre et Meuse.*

He became *chef de brigade* of the 25th Légère in 1795 and distinguished himself at the passage of the Linth in Switzerland. There followed a term of service in Italy, on the Mincio and then in the garrison of Montmédy. By 1805, he was with the French troops in Holland and then joined the *Grande Armée* as chief of staff to Marshal Mortier. The Army of Observation of the Gironde welcomed him at the outbreak of operations in Spain in 1807, where he became governor of Burgos the following year. He played a distinguished part at the Battle of Almonacíd in 1809 and joined Soult in 1811 for Albuera.

Godinot committed suicide a short time after Albuera, on 27 October. He had been sent to the lines of Gibraltar and had participated in an unfortunate expedition to Saint-Roch which had scant success and he received a rebuke of some strength from Marshal Soult. Godinot was mortified since he considered the rebuke unjust and there was a heated exchange.

> He returned to his quarters where he demanded of the sentry at his door 'Your weapon; is it loaded?' the sentry responded that it was and Godinot said 'Well, give it to me'. Then, without hesitation, he placed the butt on the floor, placed his foot on the trigger and blew his brains out before anybody had the time to stop him.[13]

Another source[14] says that the weapon was a pistol, which seems more likely if a little less dramatic. It appears that Godinot was always very susceptible to imputations against his honour and his actions indicate he took this reproach very badly.

GÉNÉRAL DE DIVISION COMTE HONORÉ THÉODORE MAXIME GAZAN

Born on 29 October 1765 in Grasse in the south of France, Gazan began to pursue a military career whilst still in his teens and became a *sous-lieutenant* of the Coast Guard Artillery at Antibes at the age of 15. Nine years later he became a full lieutenant in the grenadiers of the National Guard of Grasse with promotion to *capitaine aide-major* in 1790. At the Fête de la Fédération, in 1790, Gazan was appointed to the National Guard and promoted to lieutenant colonel of the Var Volunteers battalion the year after. Active service followed and he served in the Army of the Rhine and Moselle, the Army of the West and the Army of Italy in the following years, achieving the rank of *général de brigade* in the Army of the Danube in the final year of the century and then being promoted *général de division* the very same year. The following year, he participated in the defence of the city of Genoa. Thus, in nine years, Gazan had progressed from colonel of a volunteer National Guard battalion to the command of a division in the field.

There followed a quieter period until, in 1805, he was appointed to the *Armée des Côtes* (Army of the Coasts) and then to the *Grande Armée* under Marshal Lannes. When he was detached to serve as commander of the 2nd Division under Marshal Mortier, his division was effectively destroyed in the clash with the Austro-Russian force under Kutusov and Schmidt, at Dürnstein-Loiben on 11 November 1805. Gazan distinguished himself at this unfortunate affair which was caused by Mortier's failure to secure his left flank. The report on the battle included the following about Gazan: 'He had two horses shot under him in this action which merited for him, the grade "*officier de la Legion d'honneur*"'. A little under a week later, Gazan fought at Hollabrunn and Schöngraben and the previous defeat was avenged.

After this came Jena and Pultusk, followed by a posting to Spain – still under Mortier – and the horrors of the Zaragoza siege. In 1810, Gazan was appointed chief of staff of the *Armée du Midi*. In this role, he served at Albuera and remained with Soult through the Pyrenees campaign until the end of the war.

After the restoration of the monarchy, he obtained the post of inspector-general of the infantry in the north but defected when Napoleon escaped from Elba, joining the emperor at Grasse. He was forgiven by Louis at the second restoration and again became inspector-general of the infantry. He retired in 1825 and died six months short of the age of 80, in 1845 at home in Grasse.

General Marie-Victor Nicolas de Fay Latour-Maubourg

Latour-Maubourg was born in the Chateau of La Motte de Galaure, near Grenoble, on 22 May 1768. He was the youngest son of Claude Florimond de Fay de Cosse, Comte de la Tour-Maubourg, and Marie-Francoise de Vachon de Belmont, part of an old noble family dating back to the sixteenth century.

Latour-Maubourg enlisted as a *sous lieutenant* in the infantry regiment *de Beaujolais* on 15 July 1782 and, during the next ten years, gradually progressed in rank and reputation – in one adventure he assisted in saving the life of Queen Marie-Antoinette. He was appointed colonel of the 3rd Chasseurs-à-Cheval Regiment[15] on 5 February 1792 and then became colonel of the 22nd Chasseurs-à-Cheval in 1793.[16] He was serving in Belgium when the Austrians were interning prominent French officers; Latour-Maubourg was unfortunate enough to be amongst their number but his luck resurfaced and he was released a few weeks later at the end of September. It was his plan to return to France but he was ordered to Brussels as an émigré and here he remained for the next five years.

He returned to France at the end of 1799 and was almost immediately sent to Egypt by Napoleon as first consul to announce the establishment of the Consulate. At Aboukir in February 1800, General Kléber appointed him as an *aide de camp* and he was present at the fall of Belbeis. On the murder of Kléber, General Menou took command of the French and retained Latour-Maubourg in his role. He still had command of the 22nd Chasseurs-à-Cheval and, whilst at Alexandria, on 13 March 1801, he was seriously wounded in the head by an exploding shell. He returned to France with his regiment and was confirmed as *chef de brigade* of the 22nd Chasseurs-à-Cheval in July 1802.

Murat commanded the cavalry reserve at Austerlitz when Latour-Maubourg was sent with his regiment to join that corps as part of Milhaud's brigade. His regiment was present at Austerlitz, and Latour-Maubourg was promoted to *général de brigade* less than three weeks after the battle on 24 December 1805, as a result of his conduct.

This promotion took him away from the 22e Chasseurs and, in 1806, he commanded a brigade of *dragons à cheval* at the battle of Jena on 14 October, again as part of Murat's cavalry reserve. Latour-Maubourg's brigade comprised 9th and 22nd Dragoon Regiments. He remained with this same formation for Eylau on 7 February 1807. The division to which the brigade was attached lost a number of regimental commanders during this period: colonels of the 5th, 21st, 8th and 12th Dragoons were killed or wounded but Latour-Maubourg survived and promotion to *général de division* came in May 1807. Service at Heilsberg and Friedland further enhanced his reputation and standing and he was made a baron of the empire in June 1808. Later that year he was posted to Spain, under the command of Marshal Bessières, fighting at Ucles, Medellín, Talavera de la Reyna, Ocaña and a number of smaller engagements before Albuera, following which he was designated to command a division in Andalucia.

Recalled from Spain in 1812 and viewed as a commander of considerable talent and bravery, he went to Russia, where the IV Reserve Cavalry Corps, which included a total of eleven squadrons and two horse artillery batteries of Polish and other lancer regiments, plus several cuirassier units from various allied nations (Saxons, Westphalians and Poles) making another eight squadrons and a further two horse artillery batteries. Latour-Maubourg was wounded at Borodino and distinguished himself at Mojaisk; he survived the horrors of the terrible retreat and, in 1813 was decorated with the Grand Croix de la Reunion. He was present at Bautzen, Reichenbach, Goldberg, Dresden and Leipzig, where, commanding I Cavalry Corps, he lost a leg to a canon ball. A story has come down which may or may not be apocryphal but Latour-Maubourg responded to his distraught valet: 'What have you got to cry about, idiot – you have one less boot to polish in future.'

Following Napoleon's abdication, he took service with King Louis XVIII and remained loyal during the Hundred Days. He was decorated by the king a number of times and held the posts of ambassador to London in 1819 and Minister of War the following year. In this latter role, he presided over the revival of a number of Napoleonic traditions – for example, the readoption of blue uniforms and the return to a regimental structure rather than the Bourbon legions. He was a part of the judging council at the trial of Marshal Ney and voted for the death penalty for his erstwhile comrade. Latour-Maubourg died, at the age of 82, in 1850.

Britain

The rank and file of the British army, by and large, was a volunteer force. However, many of the 'volunteers' were that in name only. Large numbers were variously tricked, inveigled or simply hijacked. The application of persuasive talk by recruiting sergeants, deliberately and resplendently attired in well-tailored uniforms, coupled with large amounts of free liquor, represented a strong incentive for the recruit to 'take the King's shilling' but, once he had, he was hooked for as long as it suited His Majesty. Others, either more or less fortunate, depending on their viewpoint, joined to avoid destitution, the law and, occasionally, parents with a blunderbuss whose daughters had succumbed to a different line in persuasive talk. This gave rise to Wellington's infamous description of them as 'scum of the Earth'. Once enlisted, they were subjected to a harsh discipline, rigorous training and not a little ill-treatment. However, they received protection from the things they were endeavouring to avoid and a degree of security in terms of pay, clothing, food and shelter.

For would-be officers, things were a little different. They did not have merely to volunteer; it was also necessary for them, or their families, to stump up large sums of money to purchase a commission in the regiment of their choice if such was available. An ensign's rank was relatively inexpensive, whilst higher ranks required progressively more funds. Uniforms and equipment had to be purchased and a mount was normally expected to be provided by even a junior officer. This meant that the officers, unlike the men, received little training and were expected to know their business from private study and talking to their more experienced colleagues. Strangely, it was a system which appeared to work and many deeds of selflessness, bravery and even tactical dexterity were evidenced many times over when the army went on campaign.

Most infantry regiments had one or two battalions considered available to take the field, whilst a third (even, rarely, a fourth) was occasionally retained to arrange recruiting and training at home. In order to ensure the security of the British Isles themselves, there were many militia and yeoman units which were not theoretically available for overseas service. However, with the advent of the Peninsular War, this status was subject to modification. There were thus quite large numbers of trained men available for the line whilst, at the camp at Shorncliffe in Kent, light infantry received the excellent training which made the light brigade (later light division) such a formidable force under 'Black Bob' Crawfurd's inspirational leadership. There was little of a similar nature in any of the other continental armies of the period.

Infantry battalions consisted of ten companies. In line battalions there was a light company, a grenadier company and eight centre companies. The light company was made up of the most agile and intelligent soldiers who would act as advance guards and flank protection, and stood on the left of the line, whilst the grenadiers consisted of the most physically imposing men and would be drawn up on the right. There were different establishments in place but in general a battalion at full strength numbered about 1,000 officers and men, although only the guards and newly landed units were ever able to field this level of strength. A good battlefield average was 700 but was more often lower, as will be seen from the Albuera Order of Battle in Appendix 1; once a unit got down to 200 or 300, it was either amalgamated with another understrength unit or sent home to recruit.

The British Army being the British Army, there were some regimental differences. The three fusilier battalions did not have individual grenadier companies as all companies except the light were considered to be grenadiers, whilst the two Kings German Legion Light battalions had all light companies.

Up to this point we have omitted any mention of the 5/60th (Royal American Regiment). The first unit in the army to be completely equipped with rifles, Wellington had decided to attach individual companies to his British infantry brigades from May 1809 in order to give them some experienced light infantry with long-range weapons. There were three companies of the regiment present at Albuera, these were attached to 2nd Division, Cole's attachment having remained at Badajoz. We have discovered no record of where these three companies were during the battle and since their casualties amounted to only 21, we suspect they were engaged in skirmishing activities on the banks of the Chicapierna.[17] Wellington had also issued a general order in 1809 that, in action, the light companies in each brigade (including the 5/60th) were to be concentrated into a small composite battalion under a field officer – this is evidenced in the light companies which formed up on the right of the 4th Division as they advanced to meet Werlé.

The cavalry operated on a similar system but were mainly recruited from the countryside rather than the towns and cities – for fairly obvious reasons. The ordinary troopers were trained both in manoeuvres and weaponry as well as the control of their mounts in noisy and stressful situations of the type they would meet on the battlefield but the officers were, once again, not recruited for their abilities but on the basis of their families' purses. The quality of that essential element, the horses, was probably one of the best in the world at that time and, generally, these beasts were well looked after both at home and on campaign.

The three British cavalry regiments – 3rd Dragoon Guards, 4th Dragoons and 13th Light Dragoons – with Beresford comprised a very small force, but it was all that could be spared when Wellington himself was badly outnumbered in this arm. The two heavy regiments were veterans of Talavera, whilst the 13th had landed in Portugal in April 1810. This last unit had incurred Beresford's ire for the way it had apparently showed a lack of discipline at Campo Mayor on 25 March 1811, although this has been recently questioned by a modern history on the British mounted arm.[18] The three British cavalry regiments present with Beresford were organized in troops and squadrons, with two

71

troops to a squadron and three squadrons to the regiment. Unlike the infantry, there was no uniform or duty differentiation between troops or squadrons, although in theory, light regiments were expected to be more proficient at scouting and patrols than the heavier units.

Artillery was probably the best-trained arm of the army, its officers usually having formal engineering training and qualifications. It was divided into the Royal Artillery (foot or field artillery) and the Royal Horse Artillery. There was also a corps of engineers to oversee siegework, bridge and road building and to direct mining and sapping activities as required. A good idea of the artillery's individual unit structure is shown in those which served with Beresford at Albuera. He had four units of British and German artillery attached, under the overall command of Major Julius Hartman: D Troop, Royal Horse Artillery under Captain Lefebure, with four 6-pounders,[19] attached to the cavalry; 1/4th Company, Royal Artillery under Captain Hawker with four 9-pounders,[20] attached to 2nd Division; 2nd company, King's German Artillery, under Captain von Cleeve with five 6-pounders and one 5.5 inch howitzer, attached to 2nd Division; 4th Company, King's German Artillery, under Captain Sympher, with five 6-pounders and one 5.5 inch howitzer, attached to 4th Division. These dispositions were adjusted during the battle as circumstances dictated.

In May 1809, between the close of the Oporto campaign and the opening of that of Talavera, Sir Arthur Wellesley organized his expeditionary British army from a collection of brigades into four infantry and one cavalry division. Although reinforcements meant that he was able to eventually increase these to eight (plus one all-Portuguese) infantry divisions and two (eventually one large) cavalry divisions, Beresford was given arguably two of the best for the siege of Badajoz and to lead on to Albuera.

The 2nd Division had been commanded by Major General (later Lieutenant General) Sir Rowland Hill since its formation and, but for his absence in England on sick leave over the winter of 1810–11, would have been under his command at Albuera, possibly with less destructive results. Indeed, it is possible that Hill would have commanded the Allied army in Beresford's place had any difficulties over seniority been resolved to that effect. The ten infantry battalions in 2nd Division's three brigades had been serving together since late 1809 and, even though some units were junior (2nd) battalions, the whole division was very much a veteran one having marched and fought together for some time; the 29th in particular had served from August 1808 and remained in Portugal with Cradock, whilst the 1/3rd had landed with Moore in September 1808 and only missed making Moore's retreat because it was escorting stores.

Major General Lowry Cole's 4th Division did not have the same pedigree, since only the 2/7th and 97th remained with the division from when it was formed, although the 3/27th and 1/40th had joined soon afterwards. The 1/7th had arrived from Nova Scotia in July 1810 and the 1/23rd in November the same year. The two battalions of the 7th and the 1/23rd were then brigaded together to form the Fusilier Brigade and the results of having such a 'semi-elite' formation as this would be demonstrated to Werlé on 16 May. Only the fusilier brigade came with Cole to Albuera.

Beresford's other infantry formation was British in name only, but its background perfectly encapsulated why a war of this nature was being fought. In June 1803, at the resumption of war, a French army had overrun Hanover, the head ('Elector') of this state was His Britannick Majesty King George III. Napoleon disbanded the Hanoverian army and tried to reform it for service under French standards. Instead of meekly accepting this, officers and men, in ones and twos to start with, then tens, then hundreds sought out ships to take them to England in order to enlist in an army alongside which they had spent most of the eighteenth century fighting.

By 1805, the King's German Legion consisted of two cavalry regiments (one light and one heavy), two light battalions, four line battalions and four artillery companies. The light battalions had been evacuated from Vigo having taken part in Moore's campaign of 1808, then at Walcheren, in 1809. Landing again in Portugal in March 1811, they were attached to Beresford's army as an independent brigade.

Although the regulations called for the infantry to fight in three rank lines, experience gained in North America and India showed British commanders that there were advantages in reducing it to just two (although there was still a nebulous third rank made up of sergeants, officers and drummers). Ostensibly it meant that the line was longer, but since the regulations laid down the minimum frontage a unit of a certain strength should take up, sometimes only a two-deep line would allow adherence. Whatever the reason, however, the French had learnt to respect the firepower of a British infantry unit and found it difficult to counter when denied the opportunity to fight in the way they preferred.

MARSHALL SIR WILLIAM CARR BERESFORD

In many ways, William Carr Beresford (1768–1854) was an unlikely choice as the army commander since, except for a (ultimately unsuccessful) campaign in South America in 1806, he had not previously operated away from Wellington.

The bastard son of the Earl of Tyrone (afterwards the Marquis of Waterford), like Wellington, he had attended a military school in France before joining the 6th Foot (1st Warwickshire) at the age of 16. His father ensured his continued promotion through purchase and, by the time that Britain had entered the war against Republican France, William was serving on board warships of the Mediterranean fleet as a captain in the 69th Foot. He was present at the siege of Toulon – possibly even coming under fire by guns commanded by a certain Napoleon Bonaparte – and on Corsica, where he met Sir John Moore. With the continued expansion of the British Army, he was named lieutenant colonel of the 88th Connaught Rangers (of which, no doubt, Thomas Picton reminded him on many occasions!) and sailed with it to India and on Sir David Baird's Red Sea expedition against Napoleon's army in Egypt.

On the resumption of war, after the Peace of Amiens, Beresford, now a brigadier-general, was sent to recapture the Cape of Good Hope from the Dutch, after which he was convinced by Sir Home Popham to take a small force to Buenos Aires and capture it from the Spanish. Perhaps not surprisingly, after some initial success he was forced to surrender but managed to escape from imprisonment and get back to Britain.

In 1807 he was selected to take a force and garrison Madeira after the French army under General Andoche Junot had forced the Portuguese Royal Family to flee Lisbon for Brazil, and he took advantage of the posting to learn the language. He was then ordered to Portugal to command a brigade under Sir John Moore during the ill-fated Coruña campaign.

Included in Wellington's paper on how Portugal could be defended was a proposal to reraise the Portuguese army so that it could fight as part of a combined force under British command. With perhaps most of the more senior British generals expecting a rapid re-evacuation, Beresford, if for no other reason other than his linguistic ability, was appointed Portuguese marshal and given a selection of promoted NCOs and officers to train the resurrected units. He was also given the local rank of lieutenant general in order to command fellow British generals. The Portuguese Regency are said to have specifically asked for Beresford but there is little doubt that Wellington pushed for the appointment and secured his wish. Fortunately, there could have been little better choice as was evidenced by the subsequent performance of the Portuguese in battle.

Some of the better trained Portuguese units were available for the Oporto campaign, and Beresford was given command of one of the flanking columns. He remained in Portugal for the Talavera campaign but, by the summer of 1810, he had trained the Portuguese well enough for Wellington to consider incorporating brigades within the main field army. The standard of his training was to be amply demonstrated at Bussaco, where Portuguese units helped defeat every French attack.

When the army fell back behind the lines of Torres Vedras, Beresford continued to ensure that Portuguese units were trained and supplied; the memoirs of Benjamin D'Urban and the Dickson Manuscrupts provide ample examples of the work he was doing. However, with Rowland Hill's sick leave meaning that there was no one of sufficient rank to take command of the siege of Badajoz, Wellington sent Beresford forward. Partly this might have been due to the likelihood of cooperating with Spanish forces, where the rank of Portuguese marshal would have been recognized as important, but Massena's retreat from Santerem had caught everyone by surprise with a large number of British generals on leave. Albuera was to demonstrate Beresford's strengths (in one instance, literally) and probably too many of his weaknesses.

After Albuera, Wellington recognized that Beresford was best placed as an organizer, although he continued to accompany the army from time to time, being wounded during the night after the Battle of Salamanca. Once the war moved into Southern France, and Wellington knew that the Russians, Austrians and Prussians had crossed the Rhine, Beresford was again given a field command, being sent to proclaim the Bourbon restoration at Bordeaux and then to lead the main attack at Toulouse, the last battle of the Peninsular War.

After Napoleon's first abdication, he accompanied the Portuguese troops on their march home and continued to administer the army. During the Hundred Days, the Portuguese army supported the Spanish defending the line of the Pyrenees, but the return of the aristocracy and the Royal Family from exile meant that the nepotism that had bedevilled the army before the war again made its appearance and Beresford found himself continually sidelined or undermined until he returned to Britain in 1822.

Readers will no doubt make up their own minds on Beresford's performance on 16 May 1811, but it is worth noting that Wellington recommended to the British Government that, were anything to happen to him, Beresford should take the command.

MAJOR GENERAL THE HONOURABLE WILLIAM STEWART

The British army – and collectors of Napoleonic memoirs – owe the Honourable William Stewart (1774–1827) a great debt. Although commissioned into the 42nd Foot (Royal Highland Regiment) in 1786, he was impressed enough by the early campaigns against the French to appreciate the need for an effective British light infantry arm. He persuaded the War Office to sponsor the raising of an Experimental Rifle Corps and, as lieutenant colonel to Coote Manningham, helped develop both its training and its ethos. He then managed to save it from being disbanded once the trial period was over and ensured that the unit was taken into the line as the 95th Foot. The Rifle Regiment seems to have been a unit in which nearly every officer and man had paper and pencil permanently to hand in order to write letters and memoirs for posterity and to provide military historians with insights into the life of a soldier on campaign.

By 1803 a decision had been made to start converting existing line regiments to light infantry, with first the 52nd and then the 43rd Foot being the original units chosen. With the 95th already at Shorncliffe camp (in Kent), the nucleus of the Light Division was being formed.

Stewart was promoted to major general in April 1808 and appointed to command a Brigade of 2nd Division on 8 August 1810; as the senior brigade commander he accordingly took over from Rowland Hill when he went home on sick leave in November. Due to his rank, he obviously could not take command of the whole force, making Beresford's appointment even more sensible on the basis of the cooperation required between the Allied armies.

There is every indication from Albuera and other occasions that Stewart was out of his depth in command of a division, although he was well regarded by the men under his command and was personally brave. It is likely that Wellington's intention was that the competent Hill would keep him under a tight rein; something missing when Beresford took over. After all, with his experience in the training of light infantry, he might have been expected to be the natural replacement for the more junior Robert Craufurd, especially when 'Black Bob' returned to England during the winter of 1810–11. Possibly the explanation lies in the words used by Wellington in his comment that 'It is necessary that Stewart should be under the particular charge of somebody.'

Major General Galbraith Lowry Cole

The long-time commander of 4th Division, Galbraith Lowry Cole (1772–1842), was the second son of the 1st Earl of Enniskillen and went through the commissioned ranks at a very fast rate. He was appointed cornet in the 12th Light Dragoons at the age of 15, and was a lieutenant colonel at 22, although in the interim he had seen service in the West Indies campaign and was to see more in Eygpt.

Appointed to the command of the 1/27th (Enniskillen) Foot, in

1805, he commanded a brigade at the Battle of Maida in Italy in 1806, and was promoted to major general in 1808. Cole replaced Alexander Campbell in command of the 4th Division after the latter was wounded at Talavera and invalided home. Normally part of the main army, the 4th was present, but largely unengaged, at Bussaco and withdrew into the lines of Torres Vedras before being sent to serve under Beresford to besiege Badajoz. Left behind when the army concentrated at Albuera in order to destroy the siege stores, the 4th Division arrived late as a result of a flash flood of the Guadiana and took up a reserve position.

In the event, Cole's attack was at least to stabilize the right flank, but this was only carried out after the urging of a relatively junior staff officer. As Oman says, however, if it had failed, Cole would have taken the responsibility for it, so he exhibited supreme moral courage – something perhaps more important than physical courage. The army as a whole was to acknowledge the work of the 4th Division with the soubriquet 'The Enthusiastics'.[21]

Cole was another general officer who was well regarded by his officers and men. Wellington, when commenting on his generals' eating standards, observed that Lowry Cole 'provided the best dinners'.

MAJOR GENERAL KARL VON ALTEN

Karl von Alten (1764–1840) commanded the light infantry brigade of the King's German Legion at Albuera, and had had a very different career to the British senior officers noted above. Commissioned into the Hanoverian Guards at the age of 17, he served in the Low Countries in the early campaigns against revolutionary France until Hanover dropped out of the war.

In 1803 France invaded Hanover and disbanded the army, but Alten escaped to England and was instrumental in setting up the KGL, especially using his experience in light infantry work to form the two light battalions. He took the brigade back to Germany in 1805 and to Denmark in 1807, before being assigned to Sir John Moore's army sent to the Baltic to cooperate with the Swedes. When nothing came of this, Moore was sent to Portugal and Alten's brigade marched with the army into Spain, being evacuated via Vigo in January 1809.

After further service at Walcheren, the brigade was sent to Portugal again in 1810 and temporarily assigned to Beresford – when it fought at Albuera – until it could be transferred to the newly formed 7th Division.

On the death of Robert Craufurd at Ciudad Rodrigo in 1812, Alten was assigned to command the Light Division. This represented a significant change for the division, for there can be no argument that it lost a little of its flamboyance. On the other hand, Alten made sure that it knew it was not fighting a private war and that Wellington could be assured that it would be where he wanted it to be.

Major General William Lumley

Lumley is one of those Peninsular War generals who was not greatly written about at the time and has not enjoyed huge attention from later historians. We are therefore able to provide only a little background.

Major General William Lumley (1769–1850) was an almost exact contemporary of both Wellington and Napoleon, being born in August 1769. Originally gazetted as a cornet in a regiment of light dragoons, he went out to the Peninsula to command an infantry brigade in 2nd Division. Robert Long having fallen into Beresford's bad books for what he saw as the mishandling of the cavalry skirmish at Campo Mayor, Lumley was given temporary command of the British and Portuguese cavalry, and thus was sufficiently senior to provide guidance to the Spanish cavalry brigades as well. The decision for Lumley to replace Long had been made a few days before but the latter felt that the implementation of the decision was ill-timed since it occurred virtually as battle commenced.

Most commentators feel that Lumley made the best use of the few assets he had, keeping the more numerous French cavalry relatively quiet until the storm and providing support to the advance of Cole's 4th Division when it was critical. Lumley was invalided home shortly after the battle, never to return. This could be seen as a great potential loss to the Allied cause, as he may well have performed better than some of the cavalry generals who came out to Spain as the arm grew in strength. One might even have wished to see him in command of one of the two heavy cavalry brigades at Waterloo.

Portugal

The French Revolution and the early empire had largely passed Portugal by. True, British warships and troop convoys visited Lisbon harbour on the way to and from the Mediterranean, and again true that there had been small-scale skirmishes with Spain when she felt herself strong enough in her alliance with France to try and take some border towns, issuing threats that had, on occasion, caused Britain to station troops there. However, real conflict had been kept to the seas where Portugal still had a large and effective fleet. This all changed in 1807 when Napoleon, demanding that Portugal close her ports to British trade, threatened to depose the House of Braganza. When no answer came, an army under General Andoche Junot marched across Spain and into Portugal. The mountains and road were to prove more of an opponent than the Portuguese army, but when the tattered remnants of the French army reached Lisbon it was to see the disappearing topsails of the Portuguese fleet carrying the court and treasury to Brazil.

Junot immediately set out to administer the new acquisition and, save for sending the most effective units to form a Portuguese Legion in France, disbanded the army and sent the soldiers back to their homes. However, the size of the occupying forces, even when joined by Spanish forces looking for plums, was such that garrisons were soon restricted to the capital and the border fortresses. When the Spanish rose in revolt in May 1808, Junot was cut off from succour.

Emboldened by the apparent French weakness and the Spanish example, local *juntas* began calling ex-soldiers back to the colours and, by the time Wellington landed at Mondego Bay in August 1808, the Bishop of Oporto was able to provide several thousand soldiers. It is fair to say that Wellington was not impressed with their fighting ability, but recognized that their mustering showed a willingness to help. It was with this support in mind that he included the need for a reconstituted Portuguese army in his 1809 assessment for defending the country. Accordingly, the Portuguese Court acquiesced in making William Beresford a marshal reporting to Wellington, but with the express task of rebuilding their army.

Beresford had to start almost from basics, as the army was a typical formation of the ancien regime. The officer corps was bloated, with too many superannuated generals who had no apparent function, and with aristocratic officers with no apparent credentials for command. Nepotism was rife and the men often left to their own devices. Beresford's first task, among many, was to teach his officer corps to be officers, and the way he did this was to bring in numbers of British officers who were immediately promoted. He hoped that by thus impugning their abilities, he could spur the native officers to improve. He then translated the British drill manual into Portuguese, and promoted some deserving British NCOs to teach it to the recruits. He was successful enough for some individual units to be attached to Wellington's army for the Oporto campaign of April 1809. Only a few units took the field during the summer of 1809, principally the Loyal Lusitanian Legion, although this unit was wholly in British pay anyway.

With the French concentrating on defeating the Spanish insurrection during most of 1810, Beresford had a breathing space to bring the army up to a standard where it could reasonably stand in the battle line alongside its red-coated allies and, by September that year, brigades were attached to each of the 3rd, 4th and 5th Divisions. Individual *caçador* (light infantry) battalions were integrated into the British Light Division. In addition, a Portuguese Division of two brigades was formed, and there were several independent brigades some of which were later attached to the 2nd, 6th and 7th Divisions.

Portuguese infantry regiments consisted of two, five-company battalions, plus, if one was available, a *caçador* battalion. As each battalion could number up to 750 officers and men, and was kept up to strength through conscription, each brigade provided almost half the strength of its parent division. One company in each battalion was a grenadier company and in theory could be stripped out to form a composite battalion. There is little evidence of light companies, a mission that would normally be carried out by the units of *caçadores* anyway.

Each *caçador* battalion had an *atirador* or sharp-shooter company, armed with rifles although, given the number of these weapons provided to the Portuguese, some may have been entirely armed with them. There were originally only six such units formed, but a further six were formed in 1811 – enough to give each of the (theoretically twelve) line brigades one each.[22]

The reformed army's baptism of fire came on 27 September 1810 at Bussaco, when both Wellington's belief and Beresford's training were vindicated. Portuguese units were more than willing to stand in front of French attacks and indeed to take the fight to them. Albuera was to show that the blue-coated units were as happy to see off French cavalry as well.

In addition to the infantry, Wellington relied on Portuguese artillery units to eke out the small number of Royal or King's German Artillery companies that could be made available. There were four artillery regiments, and individual companies were used in the field. Two of these were brigaded under the command of Major Alexander Dickson as part of Hamilton's Portuguese Division. Captain Braun (who had volunteered from the King's German Artillery) had six 9-pounders and Captain Arriaga had six 6-pounders. The artillery was fully up to British training standards.

By comparison, however, the Portuguese cavalry could not be depended upon as battle cavalry. Partly this was due to the lack of suitable horses, and partly because cavalry training takes a long time. Neither Wellington nor Beresford could invest time and money in the arm, and it was therefore never given a fair trial, usually being placed well out of harm's way – in this case on an unthreatened flank.

Overall, the Portuguese army was to more than justify the time and effort put into training it, and units were to form part of the army that marched across the Iberian Peninsula to Southern France. Not for nothing would Wellington describe them as 'the fighting cocks of the army!'

Chapter Three

The Battle

Terrain

Albuera had been suggested by Wellington some time previously as the proper place to offer battle to Soult.[1] Wellington's view was that this was the 'most central and advantageous place' for the armies to collect and combine. A study of the field suggests that it is not a particularly strong defensive position in terms of the terrain, being relatively easily turned from the right and having no serious obstacles to a frontal attack.

Effectively, the town itself and some hills immediately behind it, to the west, formed the left flank of the position which Beresford took up. From the hills, running southwards, was a barely discernible ridge with a series of relatively low heights along its eight kilometre length – far too long a position to be held by an army the size of Beresford's. Consequently, wherever the army's right flank rested, it would be overlooked by a hillock at least as high as any occupied. Since the Allies expected a frontal attack from Soult's direction of march and his obvious intention of taking the road to Badajoz to relieve that place, the considerations of this part of the terrain were probably not uppermost in the generals' thoughts.

Beresford's primary consideration was to preserve his line of retreat – which any prudent commander would be expected to do – along the Badajoz and Valverde roads that led westwards from the town. Albuera itself lay on the left bank of the river bearing the same name and a stone bridge bore the road from Almendralejo across the river and through the town. There was a second, minor bridge further downstream. The river itself, below the main bridge, was a not insubstantial water course but carried little water at the time of the battle. Above the bridge, to the south, it was formed from the junction of two tributaries – the Chicapierna Brook and the more easterly and larger Nogales Brook. Between these two streams a tongue of wooded land rose to a fairly substantial height, completely obscuring the view from the east bank of the Nogales westwards and from the west bank of the Chicapierna eastwards. This moderately dense woodland followed the right bank of the Nogales Brook almost to the start of the tongue of land where it fell away to the north-east, giving way to arable land and pasture. Where the two tributaries joined and the tongue of land began to rise was given to olive groves, which continued northwards past the bridge to just in front of the town itself.

A minor watercourse, the Valdesevillas stream ran in a gentle curve from the high ground in the south behind the hills west of Albuera. None of the smaller watercourses held more than a trickle of water and only the Albuera River below the bridge represented a serious obstacle and then only to artillery. The Nogales and Chicapierna Brooks could be crossed by all arms above their joining place.

About 2.5 kilometres southwards from the town, along the Almendral road and some 800 metres west of it, was a short (800 m) east–west ridge and it was here that Ruty sited the French guns. These guns were ably to play on the Spanish second position (sometimes referred to as 'The Fatal Hill') – a second east–west ridge about 550 metres north of the first one. Between these ridges is a flattish dip about a kilometre wide. It was here that the French V Corps would meet their fate.

Deployment

INTRODUCTION

There are many versions of what took place both before and during the Battle of Albuera and controversy raged in the early

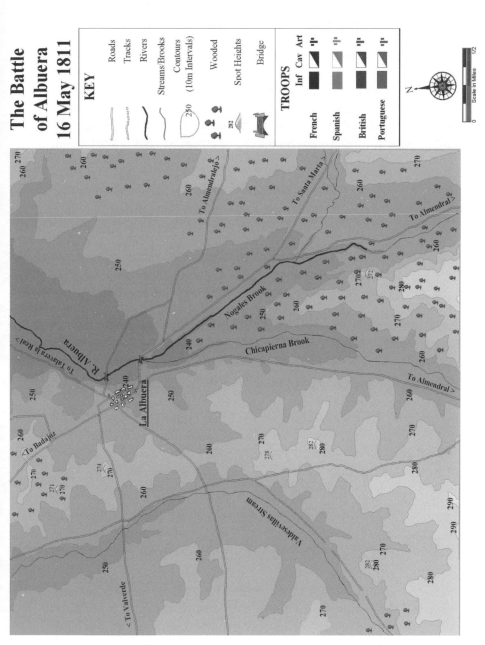

The Albuera battlefield – Terrain

1830s following the publication of Col. William Napier's massive *History of the War in the Peninsula.* His treatment of Beresford was harsh and prompted the publication of pamphlets by an anonymous supporter (believed by many to be Beresford himself but later suggested to be Sir Benjamin D'Urban, although no firm evidence is currently available as to the true identity of the writer) refuting many of the statements and contentions made by Napier about the marshal's preparation for and conduct of and in the battle. The following chapter derives some of its content from these pamphlets, which we frequently use to represent Beresford's version of what took place. Obviously, one cannot take a participant's uncontested word for everything and must always bear in mind that there will be lapses of memory, embellishments and inaccuracies. However, we have adopted the policy of using only reports, memoirs, documents, letters, etc. from those actually present to give the description of the battle some immediacy and a sense of authenticity. The subsequent chapter of the book, however, will look at this interpretation in the light of other histories and examine the actions and performance of the generals.

INITIAL DISPOSITIONS

Prior to a meeting at Valverde on 13 May, there had been some discussion over who should be in overall command of the troops in any ensuing battle. Blake announced, at the meeting, his determination to fight Soult whatever the other commanders decided to do. He maintained that he anticipated mass desertion if his men were forced to retreat into Portugal.[2] Beresford would have been most unlikely to take Badajoz, lacking any serious artillery capability for breaching the walls, and he also felt a certain caution in confronting Soult particularly in the matter of preserving that part of the British field army under his command. However, Blake's assertions left him little choice, as to 'abandon' the Spaniard to certain defeat would have been unthinkable. Following strong representations[3] by Wellington to the Spanish commanders, Castaños as senior officer by virtue of his rank of captain general 'resigned the command of the few troops of the fifth army that were present to General Blake and remained, himself, on the field of battle as a private individual'.[4] Castaños had further obtained

The Battle of Albuera 16 May 1811

KEY

Roads	
Tracks	
Rivers	
Streams/Brooks	
Contours (10m Intervals)	250
Wooded	
Spot Heights	282
Bridge	

TROOPS

	Inf	Cav	Art
French			
Spanish			
British			
Portuguese			

N

Scale in Miles

0 — 1/2

Hawker

Cole (4th Div)

To Valverde

To Badajoz

Hamilton

Braun

Stewart (2nd Div)

Sympher

Cleeve

Lumley

De España

Lefebure

Zayas

Lardizabal

Ballesteros

Villemur

Loy

Penne-

Miranda

Valdesevillas Stream

Otway

Alten

La Albuera

Arriaga

R. Albuera

To Talavera la Real

Chicapierna Brook

To Almendral

Nogales Brook

Briché

Godinot

Latour-Maubourg

5th Corps

To Almendralejo

To Santa Marta

To Almendral

To Almendral

Initial Dispositions

Blake's agreement that Beresford, holding a field marshal's rank, should thus assume overall command. Despite this, Beresford was still uneasy that Blake's declaration had effectively forced him to invite a pitched battle and wrote to Wellington accordingly.[5] Nevertheless, on 13 May, the various troops began their preparations and marches to take up their agreed positions. The time settled for this to take place was before noon on 15 May. Soult's army was at Caldezilla, Zafra and Los Santos, closely watched by Allied cavalry, under General Long, who received instructions to fall back gradually on the Albuera position.[6]

The British and Portuguese infantry, with some prearranged exceptions to ensure that the Badajoz garrison believed the besieging force was still in place, took up their positions from about noon on 15 May: Alten's KGL brigade occupied the town and bridge area of Albuera itself whilst Stewart's 2nd British division drew up in a single line between the Valverde and Badajoz roads, about a kilometre behind the town. Their right was placed upon a conical hill north-west of Albuera, whilst their left was on the high ground of the Badajoz road. Arriaga's Portuguese battery was placed on a hill that commanded the approaches to the village and the bridge. Shortly before Stewart arrived at the position – around 14.00 hours – Long had appeared, having retired somewhat precipitately, according to Beresford and D'Urban; with him were the 13th Light Dragoons, Otway's small command, which incorporated some of the Portuguese dragoons from the detached brigade of General Madden,[7] who was scouting towards Talavera la Real, some 10 miles to the north, de Grey's and Penne-Villemur's cavalry. Long claimed he had been pursued by the French who were pressing him hotly and, though his instructions were to march to Albuera, he was criticized for not disputing the retirement more resolutely and abandoning the east bank to the enemy too easily. The orders to Long came from D'Urban himself, via Colonel Rooke, the adjutant-general: 'B. General Long will march immediately to Albuera . . .'[8] Long had a running dispute with Beresford over events occurring some weeks earlier at Campo Mayor and did not enjoy cordial relations with the marshal. It had been decided to replace Long in command of the Allied cavalry and this was implemented at or shortly before the battle itself commenced.[9] Long saw this – particularly in terms of the timing – as a huge slight on his character and, indeed, it is possible he had cause for this, but there is ample evidence that the decision was taken the day previously as a means of addressing seniority amongst the various Allied cavalry brigadiers.[10] The choice of Lumley, who was a cavalry man but had been in charge of a 2nd Division infantry brigade, as a replacement was an excellent one, as he was to prove, and Long served him well during the battle.

To Stewart's left, Hamilton's Portuguese division was drawn up in line, with Collins's Independent brigade, also in line, to his rear forming the second line and reserve. Otway's light dragoons were sent to patrol the river bank and guard the army's left flank. The rest of Long's command was instructed to occupy the ground to the right of Stewart's division until the Spanish armies got there. Cole's 4th Division, when it arrived from Badajoz, was to form up behind Stewart, as the Allied second line of defence. Since it was the objective of the French to relieve Badajoz, the arrangements made by Beresford with these dispositions covered, with the best troops, the road the French marshal must take to achieve his goal. Should a retreat prove necessary, Beresford felt he had also protected his route to Valverde.

Castaños' Spanish 5th Army, under Carlos de España, together with General Cole, were not due to march from Badajoz until 02.00 hours on 16 May and, as a result, would not be there until around 08.00. Blake, however, had promised to arrive by noon on 15 May but there was no sign of him by dusk and an anxious message was dispatched for him to make all haste, the carrier having instructions to show the Spaniard the position his troops were to occupy. In the event, Blake's army did not reach the ground until 23.00 hours and did not take up their correct positions, being much closer to the river than was intended. As a result, the cavalry they replaced were tired and could not stand down until much later than they should have. The last of Blake's men did not arrive until 03.00 on 16 May and it was only when a threatening, overcast day broke that the misplacement of the Spanish became fully evident and frantic efforts were made to reposition them further back behind the slope in the positions

D'Urban had had marked out. Burriel's description of the positioning of Loy's cavalry describes exactly the appearance of the terrain there:

> The cavalry [of the Expeditionary Force from Cádiz] faced the two small hillocks which are as it were the extremity of the slope in that area, from which the right flank of the infantry was a long gun shot away. The bloodiest scene of the battle was on these two low hills . . .[11]

When Cole arrived with de España, he took up his position behind Stewart whilst Carlos de España, placed under the command of José Zayas,[12] went to support Blake and occupied a position just to the front of Ballasteros.

General Briché, following up the Allied cavalry on 15 May, was able to take possession of the east bank of the Nogales Brook with no opposition and made attempts to observe the activities of Beresford's troops. As a result of the forested tongue of land between the Nogales and Chicapierna Brooks, his view was limited. Additionally, the positioning of much of the Allied army

---

Key to all the maps showing the locations and movements of Spanish troops (numbering taken from a map produced by the Spanish General Staff after the battle).

British infantry and Allied artillery units are labelled with their battalion identities or names. Identity of individual French infantry and artillery units uncertain. In all cases, cavalry fought in their brigade formations.

1. Rgto de Murcia	2. Bón. Fijo Milicia Provincial de Canarias
3. 2° Rgto de León	4. Cazadores Reunidas
5. Rgto Ligero de Campo Mayor	6. 1° Bón Prov. Compañias de Catalanes
7. Rgto de 2° Cazadores de Barbastro	8. Rgto de Pravia
9. Rgto de Lena	10. Rgto de Castropol
11. Rgto de Cangas de Tineo	12. Rgto de Infiesto
13. Zapadores	14. 2° Bón Real Guardias de España
15. 4° Bón Real Guardias de España	16. Rgto de Irlanda
17. Rgto Veteranos de la Patria	18. Rgto Imperiales de Toledo
19. Legión de Voluntarios Extranjeros	20. Rgto de Ciudad Rodrigo
21. 1° Bón de Reales Guardias Walonas	22. Zapadores y Guias
23. Rgto Inmemorial del Rey	24. Rgto de Zamora
25. Rgto Voluntarios de Navarra	

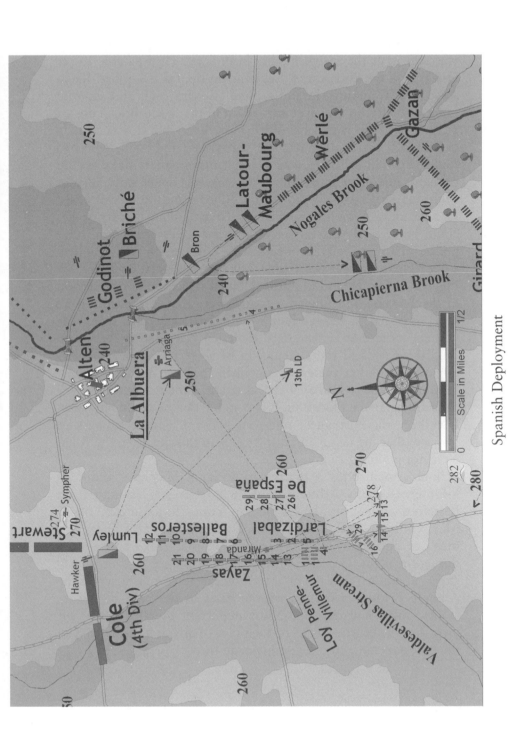

Spanish Deployment

was such that they were hidden from sight. He was able to see Otway and his Portuguese dragoons on the far left Allied flank, Alten's KGL infantry in and around Albuera itself and some of Long's cavalry on the level area south of the town. Briché posted picquets to keep watch on Allied movements but it was already evident that the Spanish had not yet arrived and Soult, who had joined his subordinate, was of the opinion that Blake would probably not arrive by the time the battle was under way. The rest of the marshal's appreciation of the Allied dispositions was based on logic and common sense. Since the two flanking cavalry bodies could be seen, it was fairly certain that Beresford would have placed his main body between them but exactly where and in what formations was not visible. His first thoughts, on seeing the English 'in line behind the little Albuera river, at the intersection of the Badajoz and Olivença roads' were that 'the enemy were [not] disposed to receive battle there. I thought that there was nothing more than a rearguard there, covering the retreat of an English army and the evacuation of siege materiel.'[13] This is obviously an 'after the event' statement because he could almost certainly not have seen Stewart's division, although he might well have anticipated its location. It is possible that he could have seen Hamilton, the Portuguese uniforms perhaps lending strength to his view that, by using 'inferior' troops in this position, the Allies were not planning to give battle.

Soult's main body was camped at Santa Martha – about 25 kilometres from Albuera and, whatever his thoughts on Beresford's intentions, he set them in motion at midnight[14] on 15 May. On his arrival, Soult reviewed the situation at Albuera and must, at this point, have become aware that Blake had arrived during the night. He determined not to do as Beresford obviously expected and make his main attack on the allied centre across the Albuera Bridge. However, on the basis of the plan his astute tactical mind had devised, it was important he reinforced their view that the centre was to be the point of attack in order to gain the necessary time to develop his main thrust.

Opening Moves (8 a.m.[15])

As efforts were being made to organize Blake's army in its proper position, it must have become clear to Soult that he was now facing a considerably larger force than he had anticipated from his observations the previous evening, despite what he later wrote in his memoirs.[16] The Spanish must have been in clear view and audible, close to the bank of the stream, and it was not until early morning that their redeployment was undertaken. Soult had thought carefully about how he might get the better of Beresford and his decision to undertake the plan he conceived was exactly the right one, whether or not Blake's army was present.

Soult knew it was essential to act quickly[17] and his plan was put into execution by his subordinates without delay. At about 8 o'clock on 16 May, he launched an attack, using the brigade commanded by General Godinot, on the town where Alten was ensconced, with a skirmish line formed on either side, and supported it on the right with demonstrations by Briché's light cavalry, which kept Otway's dragoons from menacing the French infantry. Skirmisher fire broke out along the banks of the stream as Godinot's men began an attempt to cross the bridges and were resisted by the German riflemen who had positioned themselves in the olive groves on the other side of the river. Two Spanish light infantry battalions were sent down from Lardizabal's division[18] to extend the skirmish line southwards. The musketry was joined by the sound of artillery as the twelve cannon attached to Godinot's brigade to support the attack opened fire. The bridge and the road into Albuera were commanded by the Portuguese guns of Arriaga's battery under Major Alexander Dickson, from a distance estimated by him at about 650 metres (700 yards),[19] which was judged to have been 'effectual'[20] and these cannon commenced a vigorous response to the French guns. Also marching towards the town, the Allied command could see the 6,000-strong brigade commanded by General Werlé, supported by the huge mass of dragoons under Bron and Bouvier des Eclaz – over 2,000 strong.

During the early exchanges in this section of the battlefield, as Bron's brigade moved ahead of Werlé, closer to the town, a few troopers[21] from the 20ᵉ Dragons à Cheval went across the Chicapierna for a brief time and at least two platoons[22] of the Vistular Lancers made their way up the slope towards the enemy. General Long, who was still in command of the Allied cavalry, had been ordered by D'Urban, Beresford's quartermaster general, to stand the British horse down after their lengthy night-time patrol of the Spanish deployment area. The 4th Dragoons were already foraging and were rapidly recalled, whilst the 3rd Dragoon Guards were stopped by Long and set in motion to counter the French cavalry's incursion – which they duly did. There was no significant loss to either force of horsemen.

During all this activity and unseen by the Allied command, General Girard, who had been given charge of his own and General Gazan's divisions, commenced his manoeuvres to carry out the plan devised by Soult to confound the Allies. Screened by the trees on the high ground between the two brooks, Girard marched his force southwestwards from the Santa Martha road. Latour-Maubourg wheeled Bouvier des Eclaz's dragoons to their left and, joined by the unattached cavalry and the 2ᵉ Hussards from Briché's brigade, moved off in the same direction to lend support to Girard's infantry and guns. Their objective was to appear on the right flank of the Allied army, surprise them and roll them up towards their line of retreat. The fact that this flank was held by the Spanish army gave confidence to the French, since that body had proved almost impossible to manoeuvre on the fields of battle contested up to this point in time. A complete change of front would prove an extremely difficult and dangerous operation. It was shortly after 08.30 hours as the dragoons turned westwards off the road. The sky was still overcast, although occasional gaps in the clouds allowed the sun to show through from time to time.

Zayas Stands Firm (8.30–9.45)

At about this time, with thunder rumbling in the distance, Col. von Schepeler turned his telescope to the right of the enemy's position. Until recently a major in the corps of the Duke of Brunswick-Oels in England, von Schepeler, now attached to

General Zayas's headquarters, had had some experience whilst in Switzerland of Marshal Soult's penchant for the unexpected. His suspicion that the marshal's attack on Albuera town and his manoeuvres against the Allied right were merely diversions was suddenly confirmed.

A momentary glint of sunlight, reflected from thousands of French bayonets marching through the wooded hills just across the valley of the Arroyo de Chicapierna, towards his right, was unmistakable. These were the men of the divisions of Generals Girard and Gazan. He rushed to find Zayas who was in the process of taking breakfast: 'It is from there that they come, there they attack!'[23] Von Schepeler's exclamation made all heads turn to the right. General Blake immediately sent von Schepeler off to a hill on their right and sent an aide to advise Marshal Beresford of the situation. Beresford, on his arrival, responded with instructions to Blake that a refusal of the Allied right flank should be commenced by the process of wheeling 'a part of the first and all the second line of the Spanish Army . . . at right angles to their actual front'.[24] Zayas's command, presently in line parallel to the Arroyo, formed the second line, whilst Lardizabal and Ballesteros, to his front, formed the first. The marshal then turned his horse and rode off to issue orders to General Sir William Stewart to bring up the 2nd Division for the purpose of strengthening the Allied right against the impending attack. In the heat of the moment, Beresford's order to General Blake was apparently unclear or misunderstood and, with von Schepeler not yet returned with a report on the view from the hill, Blake, having not witnessed the movement of bayonets himself, was still concerned that he had substantial enemy forces to his front, engaged in a hot contest for access to the town. He could see Werlé's substantial brigade and Bron's supporting dragoons apparently ready to reinforce Godinot's attack. In consequence he only ordered Zayas to wheel one brigade to face the threatened flank. An aide was sent to Beresford explaining this and requesting clarification. As a result, a second instruction had to be issued by the marshal that the original orders should be executed. Von Schepeler who, signalling frantically, had tried unsuccessfully to attract the attention of the group of officers where he had left General Blake then set out to find him and met up with the marshal. Beresford had been unable to locate Blake whom he 'neither saw, nor heard any thing more of till after the conclusion of the battle'[25] and therefore 'proceeded to the threatened point'[26] in the company of von Schepeler;[27] he was not best pleased that his instructions had apparently been ignored.

French chasseurs from the unattached cavalry brigade had appeared without warning from the trees about 1,500 metres from where General Zayas's 4th Division was in its refused flank formation. Zayas, on his own initiative, in the absence of specific instructions from Blake to advance, had put four battalions[28] in march for the hill where von Schepeler had gone to scout the enemy activity – it was a feature which overlooked the field in the direction of the French advance.

The march was something over half a mile and, by the time Beresford arrived at the hill, Zayas had started to deploy his men in two lines facing the threat, the two battalions of guards in the first line and the regiments of Irlanda and Voluntarios de Navarra (both in column) behind them and slightly *en potence*. Miranda's six guns were with the columns. General Francisco Ballesteros was, by now, also arriving with his Spanish division to take up a position on Zayas's left. Beresford personally oversaw the dispositions of these troops.[29] Meanwhile, Girard's infantry had debouched from the wood and had commenced the process of deploying into the formation which their commander had determined upon for the attack. Ten guns of French horse artillery were being set up on a small ridge about 500 metres south of the Allied hill. Soon the shot would be flying and an assault mounted – time was running short for the Spanish to secure their position.

The French chasseurs, by now reinforced by other horsemen, had moved further to the right of the new Spanish position. General Loy, commander of the Spanish cavalry, on the high ground near the Valdesevillas (or Rivilla) stream, which ran a few hundred yards to the rear of the main Allied line, was outnumbered and his men made up of various regiments, none present in any substantial strength. The Spanish squadrons would be unable to contend with their adversaries and so he ordered a retirement, giving ground to the Frenchmen but staying in

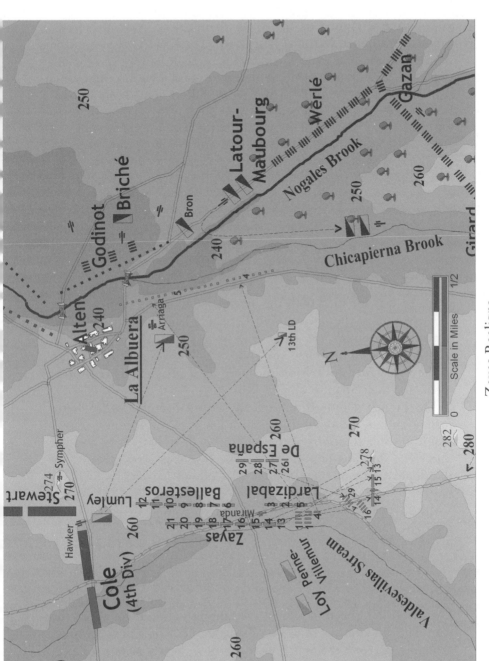

Zayas Realigns

supporting distance of the Spanish infantry. Von Schepeler pointed this out to Marshal Beresford: 'The French are supported here by cavalry and a successful attack on their battery and the hill could split the French Army. It would be good if we also had some squadrons in the centre.'[30] This might, indeed, have been a possibility, for the French horse were some distance from their infantry who, in turn, were still deploying from column of march – a formation highly vulnerable to cavalry attack. Loy's Spanish cavalry would, however, have been quite unable to fulfil this role.

Beresford, being unable to find Blake, remained with the Spanish, indicating the positions to which each of the six battalions of Ballesteros's and Lardizabal's[31] divisions should go as they arrived in support to the left of Zayas's infantry. Fortunately for the Allies, their flank was now held by the best Spanish troops on the field: battalions that had been drilled and trained for months in the camp near Cádiz on the Isla de León by Zayas himself.[32] Once he was satisfied with the arrangements being implemented, to the sound of the opening musket shots from French *tirailleurs* advancing towards the front line of the Spanish position, the marshal wheeled his horse and rode rapidly away in the direction of Stewart's British division to hurry their progress as reinforcements for their Spanish allies.

The French deployed majestically into a complex *ordre mixte* formation but, although the Spanish line was still forming, Zayas would be able to confront them with his three battalions and the one from de España's division. The line was strengthened by the deployment of the six guns of Colonel Miranda's artillery battery. The two guards battalions deployed in line, whilst the Voluntarios de Navarra and Patria remained in column on the right flank and a little to the rear.[33] The 2nd Guards battalion was formed originally from remnants of the old Royal Guard regiments that had escaped from Barcelona[34] in the early days of the war, now liberally sprinkled with other recruits but nonetheless with a great sense of pride and, by now, much experience. Both formations had been in almost continuous action throughout the war. The 4th Guards, raised on 7 August 1808 as a new regiment around a cadre of the guard were, by now, nearly as much a part of the parent body as the other guard battalion. The Regt of

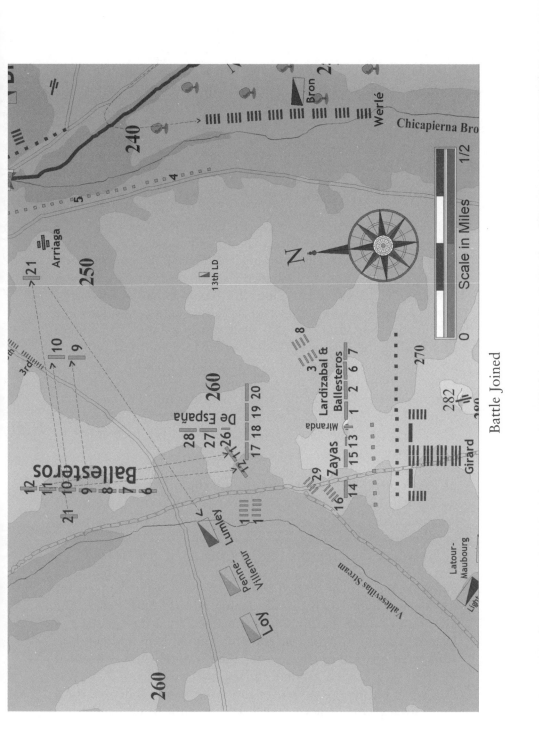

Battle Joined

Irlanda had been, in days gone by, a proud home for Irish refugees, come to fight for a fellow Catholic nation against the British who had been enemies to both. By the time of Albuera, most of Irlanda's effectives were native Spaniards but they were a seasoned battalion. Behind these four units, witnessing a now steady advance of the huge mass of French soldiery, chanting their mantras of 'En avant, en avant!', 'Vive l'Empereur!', 'A la baionette!' and marching to the staccato drumbeat of the *pas-de-charge*, was a scene of frantic activity as the other Spanish battalions manoeuvred into place to the left of Zayas's men.

The French formation which Girard had chosen was a version of one much favoured by the emperor himself. The *ordre mixte* was so-called because it combined the firepower of battalions in line with the density of battalions in column. In its simplest form, it was comprised of a number of battalions in a continuous line with further battalions on each flank but in column. In addition to providing the best of both close order formations, it provided an effective protection from cavalry flank attacks, especially whilst the body was marching. The flanking columns were able to turn their outer files to a flank and their rear ranks to face backwards, thereby providing almost as much protection as a square. The added firepower of the lines was a powerful disincentive to enemy horsemen.

The actual formation employed by Girard's own division was of four central battalions, one behind the other, in column of double companies (i.e. column of divisions). On either flank was a battalion deployed in a three-rank line, with a further battalion in column on either flank. The whole resembled a vast T.

Preceding the French columns came their *tirailleurs* in an extended order skirmish line[35] to thin the ranks of Spanish officers and tease the lines of formed troops. Soon the order rang out for the Spanish light companies to deploy into skirmish order. The agile men of these sharpshooter companies, from the Guards and Irlanda battalions, acting in twos for mutual help and support, scampered forward to confront the French skirmishers who could be seen, on the open ground, moving towards them. There was little cover for the skirmishers of either side and so it needed some nerve on the part of both French and Spanish to undertake this activity. The appearance of steady Spanish skirmishers obviously prepared to challenge them for the advantage gave pause to the French. How could this be? Previous experience had taught them that the Spanish were not capable of serious effort in this discipline. Yet now not only did these Spaniards deploy with some degree of expertise but were advancing and trading shots in what soon became a sharp fight.

As another roll of distant thunder rumbled like muted cannon fire, the French skirmishers were pushed back to their supporting companies both by the light companies of Zayas's battalions and by some controlled bayonet charges from Ballesteros,[36] where fresh files were sent to join and support their comrades, in turn pushing the enemy back towards their own lines. This contest continued back and forth for some time, during which artillery supporting Girard's division arrived, replacing the original horse battery which rejoined Latour-Maubourg's cavalry, and commenced a destructive fire on the Spanish line from the low ridge to the south. Suddenly, a gap opened in the French skirmish screen as the *tirailleurs*, moving to their left and right, cleared a path for the main body to pass through and attack the Spanish line – still only four battalions strong. This would be the reckoning!

Most of the French infantrymen had met and all had heard about this Spanish rabble: they would not stand. The columns, becoming somewhat compressed, marched forward: Girard's 1st division followed, at no great distance, by the four huge columns of Gazan's 2nd, ten battalions strong. No response materialized from the Spaniards until, at long pistol shot, the voice of the commander of the 4th Guards, Colonel Diego Ulloa,[37] rang out: '¡Batallón tiré!' and the muskets of a full battalion crashed a volley into the massed French ranks, rapidly followed by volleys from the other battalions. With a shudder, Girard's men came to a halt some distance down the slope of the hill from the Spanish. The intervals between the companies gradually disappeared and men became crowded into the restricted space of the shallow depression between the two hills. Orders were shouted and French muskets were raised. From the entire French front, musketry fire was returned against the Spanish. The bloodbath had begun.

Because of their position in the dip between the Spanish hill and the high ground where their artillery was positioned, many more of the crowded ranks of French infantry could bring their muskets to bear than would otherwise have been the case. This, coupled with the artillery bombardment, caused substantial casualties amongst Zayas's troops. However, by a fortunate circumstance, Irlanda, now deployed, found itself able to move on to the flank of Girard's formation whilst across, on the other side, units from Lardizabal's and Ballasteros's divisions had also begun outflanking the French and the slaughter became awful to witness. Both sides were now in a killing match. Neither had the impetus to advance and the Spanish height advantage was somewhat nullified by the number of French muskets that could be brought to bear. Artillery was giving close support to both sides and dense clouds of smoke billowed across the slopes of the hill, obscuring the enemy from view.

Stewart Counter-Attacks (9.45–10.30)

Stewart's men, encouraged forward by Beresford, had some two kilometres to cover in a drizzling, chilly rain before they reached the hill, where the sounds of battle had become louder and more insistent. Moving at the double, the ranks became disordered and the battalions arrived without time to make the realignments and formal deployment that their training and drill manuals prescribed. As they took up position to the right and rear of Zayas's men, the British found themselves 'clubbed'.[38] The grenadier company of the Buffs, who were at the front of the column, arrived at Zayas's position first and, urged forward by Stewart, began mounting the hill to join their immediate right flank. Following companies extended this flank as they formed line, placing the grenadiers on the extreme left of the battalion. A protégé of General Stewart remarked that he watched with horror as his patron seemed to ignore all military prudence and sent his battalions into the fray in disorder:

> It is true the Buffs were awfully mauled at Albuera, but what did my kind patron, Sir William Stewart, order them to do? They were in open column of companies right [grenadier

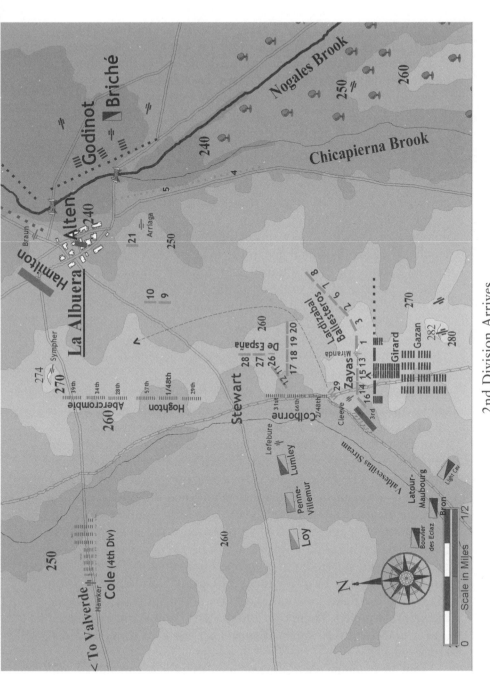

2nd Division Arrives

company] in front, and it was necessary at once to deploy into line, which Sir William with his light 95th had been accustomed to do[39] on any company: he orders them, therefore, to deploy on the Grenadiers; by this the right would become the left, what in common parlance is termed 'clubbed'; and while he was doing this, he kept advancing the Grenadiers. It is impossible to imagine a battalion in a more helpless position, and it never can be cited as any criterion that a battalion must be in squares to resist cavalry.[40]

Having taken over the brigade from Lumley after his move to the command of the cavalry, Colonel Colborne, seeing the large numbers of French cavalry menacing his brigade's advance, had requested of his divisional general that he be allowed to place his men in column or even square[41] as a counter. Stewart, however, possibly because of the urgency instilled in him by Beresford and the sight of the terrible damage being done to the Spanish, refused the request and ordered the brigade forward in the best order they could muster. They deployed into line as they arrived in position. The situation was certainly desperate but the decision was to prove a fateful one.

As they arrived, the leftmost British battalions passed through the Spanish ranks and on to the flanks of the French mass, as their line extended down the right of the hill and angled inwards. They were immediately assaulted by cannon fire and, as they delivered their first withering volleys into Girard's milling division, these hard-pressed French soldiers turned the outermost files to face their new tormentors and steadfastly returned the fire as, man by man, their casualties mounted. There was little else they could do. No means of leaving the field presented itself even had they desired to retreat, so compressed had their formation now become. The deadly contest continued unabated as Girard's men attempted to retire to allow those of Gazan's advancing division to take up the fight; inexorably, the two French divisions became inextricably mixed. There was a huge mass of humanity crammed into a comparatively small area and all sense of order had disappeared.

From threatening skies, large drops of rain began to fall and

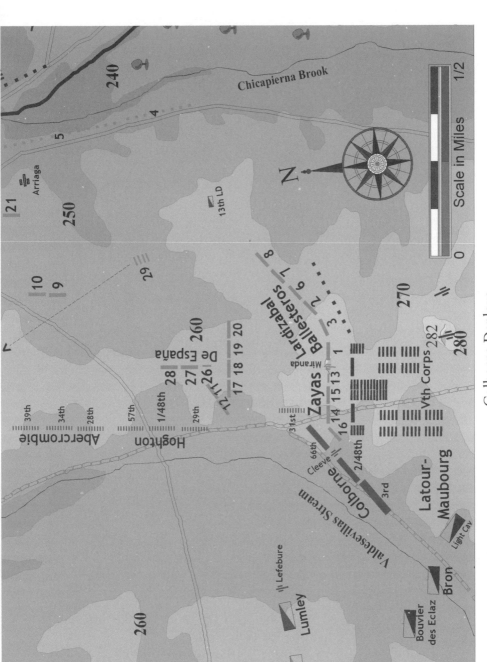

Colborne Deploys

gloom and powder smoke reduced visibility to mere yards. Suddenly, the heavens opened and the sound of musketry slackened as powder became damp in the rain and hail which sheeted down. All at once, somewhere to their right, Colborne's men heard the rumble of horses' hooves. Troubled faces turned this way and that endeavouring to find the source of the noise when, from out of the smoke and rain, there appeared the fearsome sight of horsemen clad in blue and yellow bearing down on them. These horsemen were not wielding sabres but, crouched low over their horses, they were coming fast with levelled lances. The British infantry had not encountered this weapon before and momentarily thought that the horsemen might be Spanish *garrocheros*. Yellow was typically a Spanish uniform colour – Spanish Dragoons and mounted Cazadores traditionally dressed in yellow jackets – and consequently there was much confusion. From the nearby Spanish infantry, cries of 'Traitors!'[42] rang out, which tended to support the thought that these were indeed Spanish cavalry but, as the horsemen quickened their pace and drew closer to the open flank of the Buffs, the awful truth dawned. They were French!

The Charge of the Polish Lancers (10.30)

In fact, the horsemen were Polish – the lead squadron of the Lancers of the Vistula, hidden by the smoke and lashing rain, had ridden out from concealment in a small dip in the land and were riding pell-mell on to the open flank of a battalion in line and unable to make any attempt at a proper defensive formation. With blood-curdling screams, the lancers smashed into the Buffs and began a savage butchery that was without mercy and directed against the wounded as well as those unharmed. Riding down the gaps between British and Spanish battalions alike, they wreaked a terrible havoc, spearing men from behind and drawing sabres to slash and hack at their foe. The first three of Colborne's battalions were swept away like wheat before a scythe and broke into small groups desperately fighting for their lives.

Undoubtedly, many of these horsemen were drunk[43] as well as battle mad and they gave no quarter. The Buffs' young Ensign

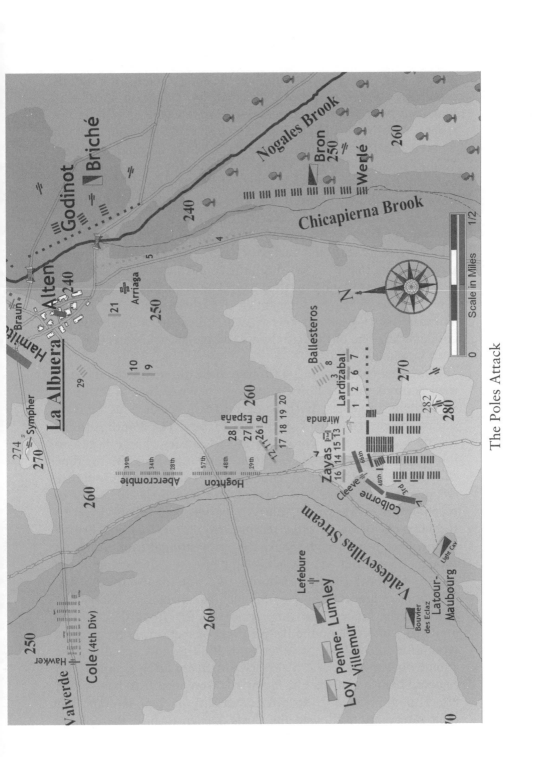

The Poles Attack

Walsh, with some difficulty holding the King's colour, the staff of which had previously been smashed by a cannon shot, was wounded by a group of lancers desperately trying to capture the trophy. Nearby, his plight was witnessed by Lieutenant Latham, who rushed to gather up the standard before it could be taken. Within seconds, Latham had received a sabre slash to the face that laid it open to the bone, taking off his nose as it did so. The next blow almost severed his arm and, as he fell, yet more weapons pierced his body. Notwithstanding his terrible injuries, the young lieutenant removed the precious flag from the remnants of its staff and tucked it safely into his jacket. Despite the dire situation in which the Buffs found themselves, they lost neither of their standards that day. The regimental colour was found on the field by a sergeant of the 7th Fusiliers after Ensign Thomas, its 16-year-old keeper, was killed defending it whilst commanding one of the battalion's companies whose captain had been wounded.

The experiences of the 2/48th were little different from those of their comrades in the Buffs. However, they were not as fortunate with their standards, both being taken in the furious fighting during the charge of the French light cavalry. The 2/66th suffered a little less than their comrades as the cavalry charge began to lose impetus but still had both their standards taken. By the time the cavalrymen reached the 2/31st, the Huntingdonshire Regiment, its square had formed and had little difficulty in repelling them. Elsewhere, Cleeve's battery had fallen victim to the lancers, losing its guns temporarily, after escaping British infantrymen ran through the battery, preventing it from firing. As soon as he realized what was taking place, in a slackening of the storm, General Lumley ordered two squadrons of the 4th Dragoons, supported by two Spanish squadrons, to charge the flank of the lancers but the supporting 2^e Hussards counter-attacked and broke up the British dragoons' effort, in the process wounding and taking prisoner both Phillips and Speeding, the squadron commanders. These two officers later escaped and rejoined their regiment. The Spaniards were unable to have much effect, possibly due to an inferior quality in their mounts, but their intervention allowed the Buffs' ensign to hide the colours

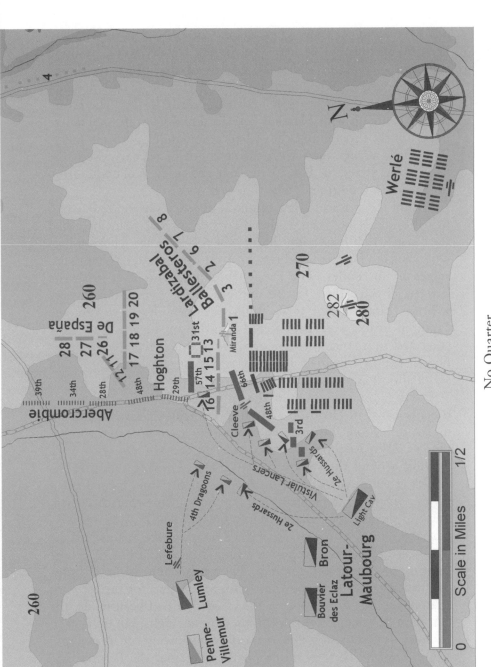

No Quarter

and gave an opportunity of escape to Colonel Colborne who had been taken prisoner earlier. The French cavalry were, by now, riding as individuals and small groups up and down the Allied lines; one large group galloped down the rear of Zayas's position and the general and his staff had temporarily to flee. The group shortly came up with Marshal Beresford and his staff, one lancer impetuously threatening the Allied commander with his lance. Beresford, a huge man with the strength of a bear, swept the lance aside, seized the Pole by his coat and threw him bodily from his saddle to the ground, where he was shot.

Within the space of a few minutes, over a thousand red-coated British soldiers had been rendered *hors de combat*. Some breathed their last in that horrifying chaos; others had received horrendous wounds from lance and sabre whilst yet others had offered themselves in surrender. The French hussars, who rode with the lancers, directed these last to the rear of the French lines where waiting infantrymen took them prisoner. If, however, the captured Briton was encountered by a lancer, he was frequently subjected to a lance thrust – even when under the charge of his French captors. Spanish losses were less severe but they would suffer shortly afterwards from the fire of their Allies.

During this slaughter in the rain, the second of Stewart's brigades, that of Hoghton arrived in the rear of Zayas's division on the hill. From this brigade, behind the main line, two companies of 29th Regiment opened fire on the lancers who were flowing around the square of the 2/31st. Hearing this fire, the 1/57th, themselves a little further down the line, loosed off a volley. Since the horsemen were, by now, somewhat dispersed, much of the musketry slammed into the backs of Zayas's infantry, partially hidden by the smoke. Heads turned and a Spanish officer was heard to cry out to his men that they should not fly whilst fighting alongside the English. The reply came from a throat parched with cartridge powder '¡No, señor, mas los Ingleses nos tirarón por atras!'[44] Realizing the error that had been made, the battalion commander of the 1/57th, Colonel Inglis, ran in front of his men, at great risk to his own safety, bellowing orders to cease firing. Despite their perilous position against the lancers, the battalion obeyed the instruction and ordered arms. At the same time, a member of Beresford's staff carried out much the same action with the 29th.

The lancers had captured, injured and killed huge numbers of British and Spanish alike and many of the prisoners were put to death after capture – harrowing tales have come down telling of the wounds inflicted and the brutality of the lancers. Indeed, as the captives were led back to the French lines, some were rescued from death by indignant French infantrymen, many of them themselves wounded. Several of the captives were later to escape but this bloodiest of battles had more twists and turns to reveal before these men could return to their regiments.

Musketry had slackened during the rain and both sides took the opportunity to draw breath. Girard, believing he had put the entire Allied army into retreat, instead of deploying, tried to replace his own division at the front of the stalled attack with that of Gazan so that he could follow up with a typical French attack in column[45] but there was so much confusion and so many dead and wounded that the process was extremely difficult; eventually, the manoeuvre was achieved but the distinction between one division and the other was impossible to determine – there was, to all appearances, simply a mass of infantry at the foot of the hill. During this process, the Allies took the opportunity to allow Zayas's men – who had suffered casualties of the order of a third of their strength without flinching – to retire in good order and to move forward the waiting battalions of Hoghton and Abercrombie. However, the lancers' charge, the damage to Colborne's command and this change of alignment had resulted in the Allied line dropping back from the crest, their position being swiftly taken up by French *tirailleurs*. At this point, a cry rang out from the French ranks, 'Now! There is nothing left but *les Gavachos*', and a general, disordered advance began. However, the Spanish under Zayas's command remained steady and gave a full discharge of musketry which threw back the French involved.[46]

The 2nd Division Renews the Firefight (11.00)

Undeterred by the sight of their fallen comrades and the appearance of French infantry on the hill, the two brigades, Abercrombie on the left and Hoghton on the right together with the gallant 31st, commenced their advance with ordered arms. The sight of this determined, grim-faced infantry steadily marching forwards caused the French skirmish line to retire to the main column and, once again, the hill was in Allied hands. The muskets of both sides – rendered unserviceable by the dampening of powder as soon as attempts were made to load weapons – were again fit for use and the awful duel could be renewed. The dressed and silent red line on the hilltop awaited the signal to continue their advance against the waiting blue-coated mass below them. Artillery fire continued unabated and brave men on both sides fell, some silently, some with anguished cries. Hoghton rode forward, raised his cocked hat and waved it vigorously; shouted orders rang out, drums beat the pace and the battalions commenced their advance. At this point, Hoghton's horse was killed and he fell, to the consternation of Beresford and his staff. However, the brigadier was shortly seen to rise, to the great relief of his comrades.[47]

In front of Abercrombie was what remained of the French skirmish line which had been bickering with Ballesteros's Spanish battalions and had climbed the hill when the Spanish retired. Soult ordered Latour-Maubourg to protect the right of his position; the cavalry commander 'received . . . from your Excellency the orders to support with the cavalry the right, where the infantry was stationed upon the height'.[48] Hoghton, on the other hand, faced Gazan's entire division. These Frenchmen, although newly placed at the front of their formation – if such is an appropriate description of the mass of men on the lower slopes of the hill – had stood and watched whilst their comrades in the 1st division were pounded by canister and roundshot from the guns of Miranda and Cleeves, peppered by the muskets of Zayas's battalions, intermittently charged by Lardizabal and Ballesteros[49] and vainly urged forwards by the thinning numbers of their officers. On their arrival at the front, they immediately received the brunt of the continuing artillery bombardment, so the appearance of 3,000 British infantry on the hilltop was a chilling sight. They had been involved in a duel with Colborne's right flank in the earlier part of the fight and were consequently not as fresh as the rest of Stewart's division. Gradually, smoke again began to obscure the

This is the so-called 'Conical Hill' which was the left flank of Sewart's initial position. Sympher's battery commanded the main road and bridge (to the right) from this position.

And this is the bridge commanded by Sympher's guns. The conical hill is several hundred yards behind the clump of trees, which hide it in this view.

A view of the bridge from upstream. The building on the centre skyline is the church, around 600 metres from the bridge. It is on a height 257 metres above sea level. The bridge is 243 metres above sea level.

This is the second bridge, downstream (north) of and seen from the main bridge. As can be seen, the Albuera River is completely dry. This bridge is between 235 and 240 metres above sea level.

This photograph shows the distance to be covered by 2nd Division when they were ordered to march to the relief of Zayas. The building just beneath the words 'Spanish Hill' was not built at the time of the battle but serves to locate the position occupied by Zayas when first confronting the French Vth Corps.

This is the ground over which the French approached the battlefield. The church can be made out almost dead centre of the photograph. The land here would have been wooded in 1811.

And this is the view in the opposite direction. The photograph is taken from the approximate first Spanish position. At the left hand end of the olive grove is the white building that can be seen in the middle ground of the previous photograph.

This photograph indicates fairly clearly that the land undulated gently and that there were no major hills or valleys. The cultivation (vines) of the ground taken up by Vth Corps was not present at the time of the battle.

Taken from the ridge where the French artillery was sited, the building in the centre is the Casa de Manzano (Apple store) which is presently not in use and was not built at the time of the battle. On the skyline towards the left edge can be made out a water tower which marks the 'Conical Hill' where Sympher's battery was positioned.

And this is the view Girard's men would have had as they approached Zayas.

This is the 'road' from Albuera that Stewart used to reach Zayas. Colborne's men would have turned left and mounted the ridge which climbs up towards the left of the photograph.

This represents an area in roughly the right place, of roughly the right size and virtually invisible from the Spanish hill that we believe was used to hide the Lancers and Hussars. However, we can not say specifically that is was the actual location.

Just off the photograph to the left was the position where Arriaga's Portuguese artillery was positioned on a slight hillock. A memorial obelisk now occupies this position. The hill forming the skyline was where Ballesteros and Lardizabal were positioned (their backs would be to the camera).

The stake-and-wire fences indicating the line of the Valdesevillas Stream and taken from roughly level with the French ridge looking northwards.

This photograph and the previous one were taken in May 2004 (all other photographs taken in September 2005), when the crops were at a different stage of development. The sky probably looks similar to the way it would have done at around 9 am. The 4th Division marched across the young cereal crop to meet Werlé somewhat to the right of the picture edge. French Dragoons attacked them for a good proportion of the march - it is ideal ground for cavalry. The skyline is the rear of the Spanish hill.

Left: the obelisk is the site of an annual service of commemoration and is located on the position where Arriaga's Portuguese battery was placed; *right:* located in the centre of the town, this is the memorial referred to in Sr Maroto's Introduction.

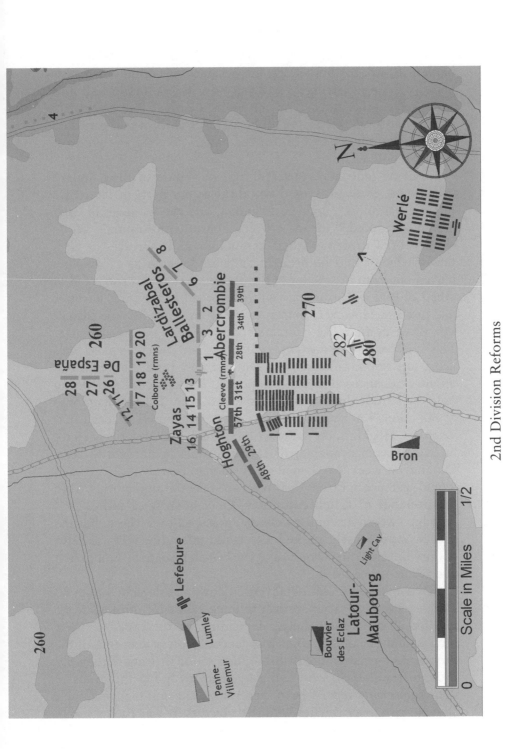

2nd Division Reforms

battlefield and, for both sides, life became one continuous night-
mare of biting cartridges, pouring powder, ramming ball and
firing off another volley. At one point, Coronel José Miranda's
battery had a munitions box hit by a French shell, which panicked
the draught animals and caused the battery to cease fire whilst it
was extinguished.[50]

Surviving redcoats, spattered with the blood of their injured
neighbours, gradually closed up on the colour party at the centre
of their battalion; numbers dwindled, and the frontage of each
battalion reduced.[51] French officers, hoarse with shouting, vainly
endeavoured to deploy their commands and increase the firepower which could be brought to bear. As soon as a company
moved out from the shelter of the one in front, it was subjected to
a hail of lead and iron and swiftly returned to the safer haven it
had just left. However, as men in the front ranks became casualties, those in the ranks behind stepped forward into their places.
This was one of the few engagements where the concept of lines
being superior to columns was demonstrably valid. As the British
infantry advanced down the slope, the French could now bring
only their front three ranks' muskets to bear. This frontage was
one of about 400 men, which gave a total fire power of just 1,200
weapons. Hoghton, on the other hand, had 2,000 relatively fresh,
unfired muskets available, all of which could be brought to bear.
On and on went the slaughter; as ammunition dwindled,[52] men
would scamper out from their places to take the ammunition from
the pouches of fallen comrades. Occasionally, a red-coated
battalion would attempt its charge, presaged by a cheer, but the
French were densely packed and could not retire very far; also
cavalry hovered menacingly, and the British repeatedly had to halt
and recommence firing.[53]

In this manner, Hoghton advanced down the slope to within 20
yards of his adversary.[54] British training called for muskets to be
levelled at different heights, depending on the range to their
targets, and the aiming point was generally lower than that of the
French. As a result, more British bullets found their mark than did
those of the French, who had a tendency to fire at the heads of
their opponents regardless of the range, causing many of their
shots to pass over the heads of their targets. It was thus a some-

what uneven contest in terms of casualties but there were far more Frenchmen than Britons and Beresford could see the gradual melting away of his precious troops.

It was not only the common soldier who suffered. In this murderous episode, Stewart and Hoghton were both twice wounded – the latter fatally. Inglis replaced Hoghton in brigade command, only to receive a round of canister in his chest. He remained with his battalion and uttered the renowned words 'Die hard, 57th, die hard!' and the regiment was thenceforth immortalized as 'The Die Hards'. Both the other battalion commanders in Hoghton's brigade received wounds.[55] In the end, fifty-six of the brigade's officers suffered injuries of varying severity. On the French side, Generals Breyer and Maransin were wounded, whilst General Pepin was killed; in all, 115 French officers in the two divisions became casualties and a further fifteen were reported missing after the battle.[56] This represents an enormous percentage of those present, testifying to the intensity of the fight. The French dead were lying in piles, preventing any forward movement and acting as a constant reminder to the survivors of what awaited them as they took their place at the front. A comprehensive casualty list is given with the orders of battle in Appendix 1.

The two commanders-in-chief now each faced their own dilemmas. Soult had Werlé's brigade, three battalions of grenadier companies and two dragoon brigades virtually untouched by the action so far. How might they be used to break the deadlock? He could see Cole's untouched 4th Division a little over a mile away guarding the Allied army's path of retreat and he knew that Hamilton's Portuguese had not yet been engaged. Whatever he might attempt would no doubt be affected by Beresford's use of these so far unengaged divisions. Although his dragoons were more numerous and of better quality than the bulk of the Allied horse, the latter were not to be dismissed lightly. Later, in his report to Berthier,[57] Soult was to say:

Positioned as I was on the high ground, I was surprised to see such large numbers of troops; and shortly thereafter I learned, from a Spanish prisoner, that Blake had arrived with

9,000 men, and joined at three in the morning. The field was no longer equal. The enemy had more than 30,000 men, whilst I had only 18,000. I decided I could no longer pursue my plan, and ordered that the enemy position we had taken should be held.

He therefore decided that his unused troops should not be used for any offensive action. Strangely, he appeared to believe he was in possession of a defensible position when, in fact, his main body was being destroyed in a hollow between two hills. He also seems to have remembered his own strength incorrectly, since his army comprised over 24,000 men and the suggestion that he had taken an enemy position was complete nonsense.

Beresford, likewise, could see that his own position at the hill was becoming untenable. The 2nd Division was disappearing before his eyes and his nearest British force was Cole's 4th Division whom he had told to remain in place at all costs to preserve the line of any retreat. Hamilton was still behind Albuera, a mile and a half distant and Godinot was engaging Alten's small force in a hot firefight. Coupled with this were the growing demands from Hoghton's men for more ammunition;[58] although these demands appeared not to reach Beresford in terms of constituting a 'failure of ammunition',[59] the supply of cartridges was almost exhausted within the ranks. Faced with what would have to be a critical decision, the marshal determined on a course of action that was to place even greater burdens on his peace of mind and expectations of the final outcome.

Beresford sent one of his aides, Col. Arbuthnot, to ride to where Hamilton was positioned and instruct him to march forthwith for the hill, then rode across to where the remaining battalions from Carlos de España's brigade stood. He ordered the two battalions of Rey and Zamora to proceed to where Hoghton and Abercrombie were in mortal combat with Gazan's infantry. The terrible noises issuing from the smoke in that direction led to an outright refusal on the part of the commanders of the two Spanish regiments and nothing Beresford tried could persuade them to budge. Worse, Arbuthnot's ride to where Hamilton had been positioned, near the conical hill west of Albuera, revealed no sign of the Portuguese troops. After some minutes spent searching for Hamilton, Arbuthnot located him close to the town where he had gone to lend assistance to Alten. He had received discretionary orders from Beresford when he was moved to Stewart's initial position and had used these orders, following a despatch from Sir Henry Hardinge,[60] to support Alten. The precious minutes lost in locating the Portuguese meant that Beresford was confronted with a situation that filled him with dismay. He desperately needed to reinforce the remains of the 2nd Division, had failed to activate the closest troops available and could discern no sign of the other formation on which he was depending. He had lost or dispatched on errands all his aides and decided he could wait for Arbuthnot no longer. Putting spurs to his horse, Beresford rode rapidly back towards Albuera to hurry the Portuguese forward.

A Timely Intervention (12.30)

Colonel Sir Henry Hardinge was deputy quartermaster-general of the Portuguese army. He had been close by Beresford's side for most of the battle but, when the marshal rode off, remained to monitor the progress of the battle raging around the hill with increasing unease. It became evident that Gazan's men, supported by the artillery on the ridge to their rear, were gradually gaining the upper hand. A mile to the north, Major General Cole could discern that all was not well with Stewart's command and wounded survivors of Colborne's brigade, making their way to the rear, had brought tidings of the combat. The noise of battle and smoke spoke amply of what could not be directly seen. Just before Beresford left to find Hamilton, Cole sent an aide, Major Roverea, to obtain orders from the Marshal. Beresford, not wishing to see his last British reserve committed, thus leaving the line of retreat compromised, issued no orders to the 4th Division. Instead, Beresford instructed Roverea to seek out one of the Spanish regiments to come to the support of the 2nd Division. The major then returned to Cole's position and almost immediately received a wound.[61] Cole continued to wait and the 2nd Division continued to suffer.

117

Hardinge became more and more concerned over the situation of Hoghton's brigade. There was little doubt that it could not hold for much longer. His mind made up, Hardinge set off to Cole's position. On his arrival, he immediately approached the 4th Division's commander and proposed to him that something must be done to succour Hoghton's men; he suggested that that something should be an immediate advance of the 4th Division. Cole now had his own dilemma. Beresford's orders had been precise and clear. Cole should remain where he was. On the other hand, the proposal made by Hardinge was clearly not something to be dismissed out of hand. He looked around him, assessing the factors which would come into play if he decided to ignore his orders and advance towards the hill. He could see the two French dragoon brigades and the remains of the light cavalry, together massing 3,500 sabres in the open ground ahead; he could call on Lumley's Allied horsemen to accompany his advance and counter the threat but was aware that, in a pitched fight, they would probably be outmatched. His own command was 5,000 strong, although more than half of these were untried Portuguese – only the Lusitanian Legion had seen combat. His mind almost made up, he rode to where Major General Lumley was waiting and they held a brief discussion about how to proceed. The die was cast. Cole and Lumley would advance together and hazard the lengthy march in the face of the French cavalry threat.

In forming up his command, Lowry Cole had to ensure that he adopted a formation which would both protect his flanks and provide adequate firepower to deter the enemy cavalry. He utilized something akin to the *ordre mixte* which Girard had adopted but made much greater use of lines and much less of columns. Myers's fusilier brigade was formed up with each battalion in echelon somewhat behind and to the right of its neighbour. On the left of this echeloned line, and using the Valdesevillas stream as a protection to their own left flank, was the battalion of the Loyal Lusitanian Legion, in column, ready to form square if the need arose. This gave protection to the fusiliers' left flank. Somewhat behind the fusiliers, and echeloned themselves, came Harvey's Portuguese brigade and on their extreme right was a 'brigade of guns'[62] and the light companies of

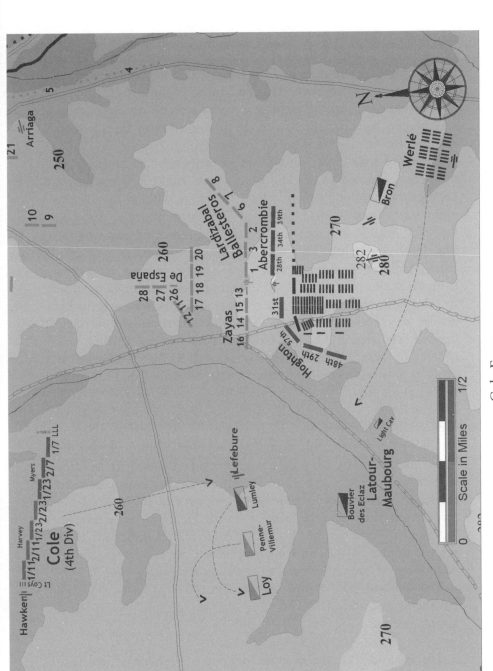

Cole Forms-up

Kemmis's brigade once more in a column, although obviously not of the same strength as that of the Lusitanian Legion. These formations were admitted by Cole himself as 'a manoeuvre always difficult to perform correctly even in a common field day'.[63] Supporting them on the right rear was Lumley's cavalry, whilst Loy placed his horsemen in front of the infantry line. In this manner, the 4th Division began its forward movement.

Beresford rode closer and closer towards Albuera and, at any moment, expected to see the blue-coated ranks of Hamilton's Portuguese marching towards him. But there was no sign of the eight battalions in that division. What the marshal did see, however, was Cole's men formed up and marching towards the bloodbath at the hill. This was contrary to his orders and, considering all that had gone before, was very unnerving. However, from his position he could do nothing to prevent it. He then began to take steps that would later be questioned as wavering in his resolve to continue the battle. Alten was instructed to extricate himself from the fight with Godinot's troops and Collins was ordered to replace Cole in his old position,[64] whilst the Portuguese artillery was instructed to 'retire by the Valverde Road, or upon the Valverde Road'.[65]

Soult now faced much the same situation as had Beresford earlier. If he did nothing, Cole's intervention, unless Latour-Maubourg's cavalry could stop them, would spell disaster for the V Corps. His idea of a defensive posture needed to be substantially modified to prevent defeat. Now was the time to commit the reserve. However, unlike Beresford, he did not suffer from recalcitrant allies or uncertainty over the location of his reserve. Sending to Werlé that he should bring his nine battalions over to the left of the hill to confront Cole, Soult then ordered Latour-Maubourg to launch his cavalry at Cole's advancing line.

The 4th and 20th Dragoons were instructed to attack Cole's advancing formation, which they did, in column,[66] with some minor success:

The 4th and 20th of Dragoons, as soon as they arrived at the eminence, made a charge upon the enemy's infantry but

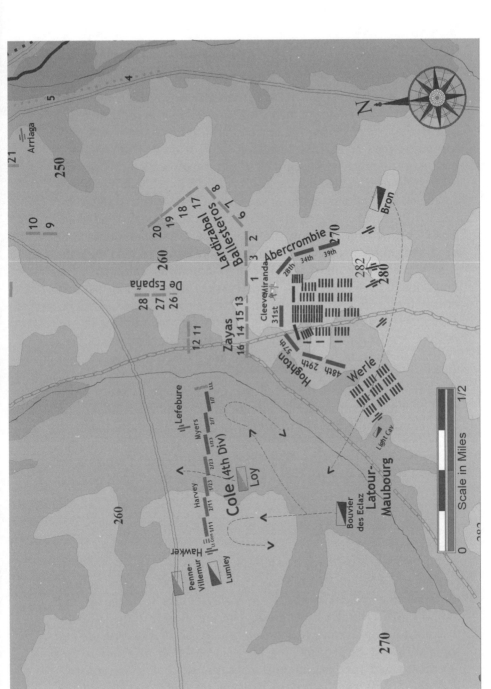

4th Division Advances

could not give full effect to it, owing to the nature of the ground and the density of the enemy's column . . .[67]

The dragoons 'sabred some and made some prisoners, though at a considerable sacrifice in men'.[68] Loy's outnumbered horsemen quickly gave way before the advancing dragoons and now Cole's formation showed that the careful consideration he had given to it before the advance had been well worth the time taken. By placing his battalions in echeloned lines, he created a depth that the French described as a column, without sacrificing firepower and the so far untried Portuguese regiments performed courageously and steadfastly throughout. During the charge, as one Portuguese unit fired, the others held their fire and so were ready to deal with the next wave of the charge whilst their comrades reloaded. The dragoons did not expect this, believing they would be able to close more effectively before the infantry had time to reload. Their charges were all repelled without their being able to close in any serious way. Lumley's command kept the right flank of Cole's division well-protected by contesting any French attempts in this direction.

As the Allied division moved inexorably towards the French, the left flank came under an intense artillery bombardment and the column of the Loyal Lusitanian Legion particularly suffered, incurring virtually all their 171 casualties in their role protecting Cole's flank. By this point, Soult had amassed most of his guns on the French ridge and they all had targets that they could engage. Cole was accompanied by Lefebure and his Royal Horse Artillery battery plus the four guns of Hawker's company which were able to assist in repelling the French cavalry from the right of Cole's formation.

While Cole, beset by the French dragoons, approached the flank of V Corps, Werlé's column crossed the ridge behind the guns and moved towards the Valdesevillas to form up and halt the 4th Division's progress. Having closely witnessed the discomfiture of Gazan's formation, would the chef de brigade opt for a different disposition for his command? It was not to be. Werlé formed into regimental columns of divisions (*colonne d'attaque*) with the battalions of each regiment one behind the other. There were thus three columns, each of two companies' frontage and a depth of nine companies.

Slowly, 4th Division began to negotiate the slope on the far side of the Valdesevillas and soon met the advancing Werlé. As a result of the formation Cole had adopted, it was the fusilier brigade and Lusitanian Legion which confronted the leading battalions of the French columns and so it was that a new and equally devastating firefight began. The British and French closed to within 50 yards[69] and commenced firing. In accordance with their drill manuals, French commanders ordered their battalions to deploy but the hail of lead emanating from the fusilier battalions discouraged the companies behind those at the front from obeying. Attempts were made during the ensuing twenty minutes to form lines but all to no avail. Notwithstanding this, those French infantrymen able to fire bravely returned like for like and were supported from their artillery on the ridge behind V Corps which ripped shot through the fusiliers and Lusitanian Legion.

The Beginning of the End (13.00 hours)

After his conversation with Cole, Hardinge rode swiftly off back to the hill where he sought out Brigadier Abercrombie and requested him to wheel his command on to the right flank of the French mass to further weaken the strength and will of the V Corps. Prior to launching Latour-Maubourg's cavalry at Cole, Soult had placed some of the French dragoons on the right of V Corps, which had kept Abercrombie in check.[70] As soon as these men were withdrawn to support their comrades against Cole's advance, Abercrombie's path was open. Hardinge's urgings were unnecessary. The brigade swung around to form their line on the right flank of V Corps, from where they poured a terrible fire into the mass of French infantry. Slowly but surely, the French gave ground and the remains of Stewart's 2nd Division advanced, firing all the while.

Having spent some time recovering composure and order, the Spanish battalions of Zayas, Lardizabal and Ballesteros now reformed a line across the entire reverse slope of the hill and began to advance towards the crest.

The Battle of Albuera 1811

At last, Beresford located Hamilton's division but was by now becoming aware that his men were in the process of prevailing at the hill. Alten, who had pulled his men out from the town preparatory to moving to Cole's old position, now received orders to retake it, which he proceeded to do: 'Several companies of 2nd light battalion, which were the nearest at hand instantly faced about and retook the village, cheering and advancing in double quick time, without meeting with any serious opposition.'[71] Brigadier Campbell's men were instructed to support. Hamilton's second brigade, commanded by Fonseca, was sent towards the hill to bolster the Allied presence there while Beresford himself now started his return to the killing ground.

The contest between the fusiliers and Werlé's brigade had developed in the same way as that between V Corps and 2nd Division. The fusilier brigade steadily advanced up the slope and steadily drove back Werlé's smoke-enshrouded infantry. Werlé himself was killed fairly early in this combat and his death served to unnerve and confuse his brigade.[72] All the while, the fusiliers' thin lines shrank, the files closing ever inward towards the colours, men were 'knocked about like skittles',[73] but the survivors still pressed doggedly on. Supported, now, on either flank by British artillery, the fusiliers gradually gained the upper hand until they suddenly became aware of a slackening in pressure. Werlé's command had suddenly given way. As the powder smoke gradually cleared, French infantrymen could be seen streaming away behind the ridge where their artillery still played on Allied targets – including Cole's dramatically shrunken formations.

Seeing their comrades fleeing the field, the mass of humanity which comprised the V Corps themselves wavered. Their fear of their situation overcame their physical inability to manoeuvre or retire in an orderly fashion. The inevitable consequence was that they joined their comrades from Werlé's brigade in a disordered retreat from the scene of their fight with what remained of Stewart's 2nd Division. Soult was dismayed. His enemy had been beaten but was too stubborn to realize it and now his own army was in full retreat. Issuing urgent orders to his artillery to continue their pounding, thereby preventing any immediate pursuit, he summoned Latour-Maubourg and instructed him to concentrate

Cole's Attack

his cavalry for the protection of the guns as they were subsequently pulled back across the Chicapierna. The three reserve grenadier battalions were now brought forward to the Chicapierna as a final means of discouraging any serious efforts by the Allies to consummate their victory.

But by about 2 or 2.30 in the afternoon, Beresford's army had given its all. Until Fonseca and Collins arrived with their Portuguese brigades, he had no fresh troops to send against Soult and, with his army firmly ensconced on the high ground and between the two streams, strong in both artillery and cavalry, the French marshal was not vulnerable even to the unused Portuguese. Nonetheless, some of the more intrepid British infantry made as if to pursue their defeated victims. Beresford was mortified and called to the 57th, who were intent on joining such a pursuit, to desist.[74] But they carried on regardless, joined by many of the Spanish units that had earlier suffered so much.

Soult covered his retreat by a combination of artillery and cavalry whilst he called up his last intact infantry formation. With so much cavalry ranged against them, the pursuing Allies were unable to press home the advance and halted on the ground previously held by Ruty's guns. Many of the erstwhile prisoners escaped during this episode and rejoined their parent units. There had been and was still to be much suffering by the wounded but the result of the battle seemed to be their main concern. A passage from von Schepeler's *History* is revealing on this matter:

I found, after the battle, a soldier of this brigade [Colborne's] fatally wounded and lying on his stomach only twenty paces from the place where the French battery had been. On being asked if he was still alive, the Englishman replied 'Yes, but who won the battle?'

'We did', I replied and he asked: 'Who is we?'

'English and Spanish'

'Ah . . . well, well.' Thus breathed a hero for the last time. Not far from Albuera, propped-up on his left arm, in a half-raised position, a French officer: the anguish of this first defeat was yet more visibly painted on his truly handsome face than that from his leg, broken by a bullet. 'You are badly wounded', I said to him, and a simple: 'Yes, sir' was his reply. At that moment, some Portugese called to me to help him up; he said, seriously, 'Thank you very much, sir'; not another word, no complaint passed his lips.

On the next day, before first light, the Allied army was under arms for fear that Soult would renew his attack. But the French had insufficient fight left in them and the rest of Kemmis's brigade arrived from Badajoz early in the morning so strengthening an army that had not been as badly mauled as their enemy. Soult made arrangements to have as many as possible of the wounded taken to Seville and left before daybreak on 18 May. Three days after the battle, the siege of Badajoz was renewed and it was clear that the Allies had gained a victory – albeit with losses, particularly to the British, that could be ill-afforded.

Chapter Four

Aftermath and Analysis

The preceding chapter provided a view of the battle largely from the words of those that took part. In the years since most of these words were written, there have been innumerable interpretations and opinions but many of the earlier histories did not have the benefit of more recently unearthed documents written by the participants themselves and their descendants.

Most recent histories indicate that Beresford made blunders, was not confident of victory and even contemplated retreat immediately before the breaking of the French infantry. Certainly, he was mortified at the loss of life and damage to his command. He was a strict disciplinarian and believed in the stoicism prevalent in the society by which he was moulded. Nevertheless, he was a compassionate man and suffered from depression in the days and weeks following the battle. He wrote to Wellington that he could 'scarcely forgive myself for risking this battle'[1] and, bearing in mind his concerns when Blake announced he would fight alone if not supported by the marshal, one can appreciate Beresford's comments, having witnessed what he did. Nevertheless his conduct of the battle was certainly not faultless.

Let us, therefore, first examine Beresford's conduct of and at the battle and endeavour to determine whether he has been harshly treated. The decision to fight was, by the marshal's own admission, taken against his better judgment, following the pressure from Blake. Should Sir William have resisted despite the statements of the Spanish general? The political and personal ramifications of such a refusal to fight would likely have caused such a rift between the Allies that it might have seriously affected their ability to prosecute the war in any sort of cooperative stance. True, Wellington would possibly have understood – his own experiences with Cuesta at Talavera two years earlier had engendered the view that the Spanish were unreliable and could not manoeuvre in the field. However, in the corridors of Westminster and the tiled *casas* of Cádiz, where dwelt the Central Junta, the mood would likely have been less understanding. Wellington had given Beresford discretionary orders which allowed him to fight a battle, and that left Beresford with the final decision. Wellington himself summed up the matter perfectly when he said: 'You could not be successful in such an action without a large loss; and we must make up our minds to affairs of this kind sometimes, or give up the game.'[2]

Having taken the decision to give battle, what of Sir William's disposition of his forces? First, we must accept that Beresford was not a Wellington. There were few, if any, on either side, other than Napoleon himself, who could be considered of anything like the calibre of the British commander-in-chief. Consequently, when criticizing Beresford, it is important to be aware of this. True, had Wellington been in command, he might well have done many things differently and received better support from both his allies and his subordinates.

On the basis of what Beresford believed, his dispositions were understandable. Soult's objective was the breaking of the siege of Badajoz and the resupply of that place. Certainly, then, the road to the fortress must be closed to the French. The town of Albuera was almost deserted. There were no roofs on the buildings, no doors or furniture – all had been used as firewood by previous French occupation – and the road itself passed through the town. This made the buildings an ideal strongpoint ahead of the main battle line. The river was not a great obstacle but was sufficient to be somewhat disruptive in its passage. As long as the position could be protected from outflanking manoeuvres, it represented a tenable defensive line in the way that the marshal intended to use it. Protection from the Allied left would be relatively simple, since the river curved eastwards just below the town and the high ground behind it gave a good view of any approach from this direction. To the right, however, things were less secure.

The gradual increase in height of successive knolls and ridges progressing to the south meant that any position taken up here was overlooked by the next piece of higher ground, giving a flank attack the advantage. The Allied army was not sufficiently strong in numbers to extend itself far enough to secure the whole of the area. If Beresford moved the entire army southwards to overcome this disadvantage, Albuera and the Badajoz road would be un-covered. Indeed, the suggestion put forward that the Allied left should have been placed where Beresford actually placed the Spanish right flank would appear, on the face of it, to be nonsense. If, perhaps, the left of Stewart's division had been posi-tioned where Beresford placed its right some advantage might have been derived, in that the high ground where Ruty positioned the French artillery and behind which V Corps formed up for the attack, would have been under Allied infantry control rather than just initially being occupied by its weaker cavalry who, in the event, were easily driven off. This could, however, have weakened the protection for the left flank and, to an extent, uncovered the road to Badajoz.

Why did Beresford place the Spanish, whom most historians (and, indeed, Beresford himself at the time[3]) would, with some justification, judge less reliable than the British, on the most open flank, in view of Soult's huge preponderance in the mounted arm? Sir William's anonymous supporter would have us believe that 'General Blake was established on the right . . . simply because he came from that flank and . . . [Beresford] considered it the strongest and least likely to be attacked'.[4] Having visited the battlefield, we would not agree that it is the strongest position but, if Beresford believed he knew Soult's mind and considered an attack here unlikely, he had some justification in placing his forces as he did. Certainly Blake came from that direction but was extremely tardy, and this may have had a larger part to play than the strength or otherwise of the position. Beresford had intended this part of the army to be behind the military crest of the position and thus concealed from the enemy. However, Blake initially occupied a forward location (and would thus almost certainly have been remarked by Soult in his reconnaissance – despite what the marshal says in his report).

It has been said that Wellington 'would have hidden his troops away and given Soult no clue as to his strength or his weak points'.[5] However, Beresford did exactly this as effectively as he could. It was Blake's late arrival that may well have given the game away about Allied deployment – and Soult denied knowledge of Blake's presence until near the end of the conflict on the Spanish hill. It is possible that Soult, in reality aware of Blake, determined on his outflanking manoeuvre at this point, entirely because he considered the Spanish less of an obstacle.

The final criticism against Beresford's dispositions is that he should have occupied the high ground between the Nogales and Chicapierna streams. Since this ground was forested at the time, it is doubtful that occupation of this tongue of land in strength would have been as effective as the proponents of such a deployment appear to suggest. Where Beresford admits to error is in not establishing light infantry in the wooded area. Such a precaution would have given inescapable evidence of Soult's intentions and gained Beresford much time.

Looking next at Beresford's conduct of the battle, one can, perhaps, be a little more critical. The first intimation that all was not well came when the outflanking manoeuvre was first detected by von Schepeler. As soon as Beresford was sure in his own mind that this was a real threat, he issued orders for the change of front. He then obviously decided that he needed to place British troops on this new front but, instead of sending an *aide* with orders to Stewart to advance with all haste to the new position, it seems the marshal went himself. Not only did he do this but it appears he rode around ordering up the individual brigades of the 2nd Division. Consequently, when Blake decided the flank attack was a sideshow, Beresford was not at the critical place to insist his orders to the Spaniard were carried out. Fortunately, General Zayas had a sound appreciation of the situation and the presence of mind to go to the flank himself. However, valuable time was lost and the marshal then had to see personally to the ordering of the Spanish formations, since Blake had disappeared from the scene.

The same kind of behaviour was evident at other stages of the battle. For example, when it became evident that the 2nd Division needed reinforcing and Beresford could not persuade Carlos de España's men to go into the line, he went off to find Hamilton. If he had, as has been reported,[6] 'no other Aides de Camp present', he might well have required Sir Henry Hardinge to seek out the Portuguese and hasten them to the critical point rather than going himself. However, had he in fact done so, one is led to wonder whether he would have issued the key order for Cole to advance along the bank of the Valdesevillas himself. It has been suggested (not least by William Napier) that Beresford had determined on retreat and orders to Alten to quit Albuera village and to Dickson to move his artillery are cited as evidence of this. However there is no direct evidence of such an intent and Beresford himself strongly denies it. Indeed, any general that did not bear in mind the possible need for retreat as an eventuality, and keep options available for its implementation, would be worthy of criticism so, whilst Beresford may have considered what should be done in the event, there is nothing specific to indicate a loss of determination to see things through.

In short, whilst Beresford may not have conducted the progress of the battle in the best manner, his personal bravery, commitment and diligence are hardly in question. A query, however, does hang over the behaviour of some of the marshal's subordinates and colleagues.

We have already raised the fact that Blake appeared to go absent shortly after he failed to implement Beresford's order to change front but, apart from Sir William saying he did not see Blake again until after the end of the battle, no mention of this absence or its reason is found. One can only surmise that the Spanish general was engaged in something relevant and essential to the battle or that, realizing his error, he had decided not to remain where he was easily located.

The Duke of Wellington commented that Beresford 'would have succeeded without much loss if the Spaniards could have moved; nevertheless there they stood like stocks, both parties firing on them, and it was necessary to apply the British every-where'.[7] Whilst much comment has been made about Beresford's failed attempts to get Carlos de España's men to reinforce the refused flank, we have encountered little mention of the failure of Ballesteros and Lardizabal to advance to threaten more immediately the right flank of V Corps. Although this may have been in Wellington's mind, his use of words seems to suggest he was referring, most unfairly, to Zayas. No criticism can be levelled at Zayas's troops in this respect; they did not make any substantial forward movement, it is true, but their very resilience in holding, unsupported, their position gave time for the arrival of Stewart and brought the French to a halt. Ballesteros and Lardizabal, however, faced 'nothing but skirmishers',[8] but seem to have made no serious moves to engage the main body. This despite the fact that, when Zayas retired to allow 2nd Division to take up their position, the British cleared the skirmishers who had arrived on the top of the hill without firing at them. Wellington does say:

> if we could have moved the Spanish army; at Albuera, the natural thing would have been to support the Spaniards on the right with the Spaniards who were next to them; but any movement of that body would have created inextricable confusion[9]

and this fairly obviously refers to Ballesteros and Lardizabal. One wonders whether Lardizabal's troops, likely to have benefited from much of the same training given to Zayas's men at the Isla de León camp, might have been successfully employed but, as we have pointed out, Beresford was not always where he might have done the most good and Blake was not on the scene, so it seems the necessary orders were not given and the two divisional commanders did not act on their own initiative.

William Stewart was the architect of his division's own downfall in hurrying battalions into the line before they were properly ordered so that their deployment prevented proper manoeuvre capability. He further refused permission for the right flanking battalion to be placed into a formation that would have enabled them to repulse the charge of the French light cavalry. From his position, it is doubtful that Beresford could have seen this and intervened but a commander-in-chief must rely on the good sense of his subordinates for such matters. Hamilton had been given discretionary orders to support Alten in the town and certainly the action had grown hotter in that location with Godinot's pressing of his attack. Consequently, he cannot be taken to task for having moved from where Beresford expected to find him. Yet it seems some of Beresford's subordinates did not provide their commander with anything like the professional competence that the situation merited.

Despite the mistakes that were made, the British infantry performed wonders and, supported by their artillery and the redoubtable Lumley, whose handling of a numerically and qualitatively inferior mounted arm was beyond reproach, both the 2nd Division and the gallant fusiliers gave their lives without conceding an inch of ground, eventually emerging victorious.

On the French side, we have already discussed Soult's appreciation of the situation when he determined his grand tactics. Whatever he knew in reality about the Allied dispositions and strength, Soult undoubtedly took the right decisions about where to attack and how to divert the Allied attention to the point where they expected the attack. It suggests he knew more about their dispositions than he admitted to, since he seems to have divined the expectation of attack against the town and fed that expectation with Godinot's feint. Soult's biggest failing was in his inability to modify and augment his plans once they were put in motion. Girard, put in charge of the main attack, made a major error in sending Gazan's division in support of his own division so early in proceedings. The two bodies became so inextricably intermixed that they prevented their brigadiers from manoeuvring appropriately and so the attack became bogged down and immovable.

Had 1st Division mounted its attack and possibly even broadened its front against the Spanish to encompass Lardizabal and Ballesteros by fully deploying into line once a firefight became inevitable and before Stewart came up, the less competent of the Spanish infantry might have given way; then, Gazan's approach to support their comrades could have settled the matter. It is doubtful that Zayas alone could have prevented this.

Additionally, the preponderance of French cavalry on their left was never fully exploited. It is likely that one of the dragoon brigades could have kept the Allied cavalry in check on the French left and the second deployed to threaten and harass the Spanish left. It seems that, for a variety of reasons, both commanders became somewhat mesmerized by the firefight occurring between the two hills and failed to take action to turn the situation. In the end, the sheer doggedness, persistence and raw courage of the British infantry and of Zayas's division wore down French resolve and eventually carried the day.

For the Spanish, there seems to be some validity in Wellington's view that the their troops were incapable of manoeuvre. Certainly this is not true of Zayas's men, who skirmished and contended with Girard perfectly ably, even if they were not required to perform complex battlefield manoeuvres. It should not have been true for Lardizabal, who had been present during the time on the Isla de León when Zayas was retraining his division. Blake's failure to make his presence felt by taking a somewhat more aggressive stance with Lardizabal and Ballesteros would not be above criticism had he been there to do so. Again, had the Spanish left moved to envelop the right flank of V Corps, it is quite possible that one of Latour-Maubourg's dragoon brigades would have been brought over to counter such a move and, without Allied cavalry to oppose it, would likely have succeeded in nullifying the attempt.

In refusing to advance to the support of their comrades, the behaviour of the battalions of de España's battalions was reprehensible in the terms under which warfare was fought in 1811 but one can have sympathy for men who had witnessed the bloodbath so close to their position and felt disinclined to add to it with their own number.

The outstanding achievement of Spanish arms on the day was undoubtedly the stand made by Zayas and his 4th Division. Without their contribution there would likely have been no time for Stewart to occupy the hill and V Corps would have been advancing to roll up the Allied flank. Lumley could have done little to prevent this with the preponderance of French cavalry confronting him and the retiring Spanish would have made it extremely difficult for Beresford to organize a solid defence in another position. Almost certainly, there would have needed to be a fighting retreat. This would likely have allowed Soult to achieve his objective of resupplying Badajoz.

In the event the marshal failed in his enterprise and, after regaining some order, covered by his still powerful artillery and cavalry, he retired from whence he came the next day, followed at a respectable distance by the Spanish and Lumley's cavalry. Almost as a footnote, as the battle came to an end, the heavens opened and a repeat of the chill rain that hid the charge of the Polish Lancers made conditions close to unbearable for the thousands of wounded who covered the shallow depression between the two hills. Bandsmen and medical staff tried to give assistance but the numbers of dead and injured were so great that there was little they could do. Many French wounded were found by the Allies in a tiny chapel that was situated in the woods beyond the Nogales Brook. Even had there been respectable medical facilities available, it is doubtful they could have coped with the numbers of dead and wounded.

Strangely, the longer term effects of such a bloody battle were negligible. Certainly the various armies involved had learned something but, even though the siege of Badajoz was quickly resumed, British engineering incompetence and the lack of proper siege artillery meant that, on 10 June 1811, Wellington raised the siege. Soult was forced back by Beresford's pursuit (not pressed especially strongly) and his cavalry severely handled by Lumley, Madden and Penne-Villemur at Usagre, but it was not Wellington's intention to invade Andalucia and the army halted. Beresford returned to Portugal to deal with problems in the Portuguese army that, in his absence, had not maintained its status well, but it was generally felt that Wellington's dissatisfaction with his Extremaduran campaign was the reason behind this departure. Rowland Hill returned from leave and was placed in command of this wing of the British forces. It had been Wellington's intention to create a new division (8th), but the heavy loss at Albuera effectively derailed this plan. Such were the main tangible results of the battle.

Appendix 1

Orders of Battle

Wherever possible, we have given the names of commanders of the various units engaged; these will be found in parentheses following the regiment name. If the commander's name is not known, we have used a question mark. Casualties are shown in brackets after the initial unit strength in the form: (killed/wounded and missing). We have used the language of the army concerned to designate ranks, units and commanders. The few translations necessary are fairly straightforward; however, some abbreviations may need clarification. In the Spanish army, Rgto is 'regiment' (*regimiento*); Bón is 'battalion' (*batallón*); M-d-C is 'major general' (*mariscal de campo*), 'ligero' is light infantry and a brigade is sometimes referred to as a *sección*. Esc is 'squadron' (Spanish *escuadrón*, French *escadron*). In the French army Ch. Btn is Chef(s) de Bataillon, Gén. Div. is Général de Division and Gén Brig. is Général de Brigade.

137

THE ALLIES
Commander-in-Chief: Field Marshal Sir William Carr Beresford

BRITISH FORCES
2nd Division (Major General Sir William Stewart)

	Officers	Men
Lieutenant Colonel John Colborne's Brigade		
1/3rd Foot – East Kent, 'The Buffs' (Lt Col Stewart)	27 (4/16)	728 (212/411)
2/31st Foot – East Surrey (Major L'Estrange)	20 (0/7)	398 (29/119)
2/48th Foot – Northamptonshire (Major Brooke)	29 (4/19)	423 (44/276)
2/66th Foot – Berkshire (Captain Binning)	24 (3/12)	417 (52/205)
Major General Daniel Hoghton's Brigade		
29th Foot – Worcestershire (Lt Col White)	31 (5/12)	476 (75/244)
1/48th Foot – Northamptonshire (Lt Col Duckworth)	33 (3/13)	464 (64/200)
1/57th Foot – West Middlesex (Colonel Inglis)	31 (2/21)	616 (87/318)
Brigadier Alexander Abercrombie's Brigade		
2/28th Foot – North Gloucestershire (Major Patterson)	28 (0/6)	491 (27/131)
2/34th Foot – Cumberland (Lt Col Fenwick)	28 (3/4)	568 (30/91)
2/39th Foot – Dorsetshire (Major Lindesay)	33 (1/4)	449 (14/79)
Divisional Light Troops		
3 Companies 5/60th Foot – Royal American (Major McMahon)	4 (0/1)	142 (2/18)
Division total	**288 (25/115)**	**5172 (636/2092)**

4th Division (Major General Galbraith Lowry Cole)

Lieutenant Colonel Sir William Myer's Brigade	*Officers*	*Men*
1/7th Foot – Royal Fusiliers (Major North)	27 (0/15)	687 (65/277)
2/7th Foot – Royal Fusiliers (Lt Col Blakeney)	28 (2/13)	540 (47/287)
1/23rd Foot – Royal Welsh Fusiliers (Lt Col Ellis)	41 (2/11)	692 (74/252)

Detached Light Cos. (from Col Kemmis's Brigade)
97th Foot – Queen's Own, 1/40th Foot –
   2nd Somersetshire, 2/27th Foot –

Enniskillen	8 (1/0)	157 (5/14)

Colonel Harvey's Portuguese Brigade	*Officers and Men*
1st & 2nd Btns 11th Regiment (Lt Col McDonnell)	1154 (0/2 off., 2/9 men)
1st & 2nd Btns 23rd Regiment (Lt Col Stubbs)	1202 (1/1 off., 3/14 men)
1st Btn Loyal Lusitanian Legion (Lt Col Hawkshaw)	572 (0/6 off., 66/99 men)
Division Total	104 (6/48) 5 004 (262/952)

Independent King's German Legion (KGL) Brigade

Major General Victor von Alten	*Officers*	*Men*
1st Light Battalion KGL (Lt Col Lenhart)	23 (0/4)	565 (4/61)
2nd Light Battalion KGL (Lt Col Halkett)	19 (1/1)	491 (3/32)
Brigade total	42 (1/5)	1056 (7/93)

Cavalry (Major General William Lumley)

Colonel de Grey's Heavy Brigade		
3rd Dragoon Gds (Col Sir Granby Calcraft)	23 (1/0)	351 (9/10)
4th Dragoons (Lt Col Leighton)	30 (0/4)	357 (3/20)
Brigade Total	53 (1/4)	708 (12/30)

Unbrigaded Light Cavalry

13th Light Dragoons (Colonel Head)	23 (0/0)	380 (0/1)

Artillery (Major Hartmann[2])	*Guns*	*Men*
D Company, Royal Horse Artillery (G Lefebure)	4 x 6 pdrs	255 (0/1 off.,
1st Co., 4th Btn, Royal Artillery (J Hawker)	4 x 9 pdrs	3/11 men)
Cleeves's Battery, KGL	5 x 6 pdrs, 1 howitzer	292 (0/2 off., 0/47 men)
Sympher's Battery, KGL	5 x 6 pdrs, 1 howitzer	
Total		547 (0/3 off., 3/58 men)

Staff: It is not known how many staff were present but 1 officer was killed and 7 wounded.

Total British casualties – all ranks and arms: 4159

PORTUGUESE FORCES
Portuguese Division (Major General Hamilton)

1st Brigade (Brig. General Campbell)	*Officers and men*
1st & 2nd Btns 4th Regiment (Lt Col Campbell)	1271 (0/1 off., 9/50 men)
1st & 2nd Btns 10th Regiment (Conde de Regende)	1119 (0/0 off., 0/11 men)
2nd Brigade (Brigadier General Fonseca)	
1st & 2nd Btns 2nd Regiment (Colonel de Costa)	1225 (0/0 off., 3/5 men)
1st & 2nd Btns 14th Regiment (Lt Col James W Oliver)	1204 (0/0 off., 0/2 men)
Division total	4819 (0/1 off., 12/68 men)

Orders of Battle

Independent Portuguese Brigade

Brigade (Colonel Collins)   *Officers and Men*
1st & 2nd Btns 5th Regiment
   (Lt Col de S Perreira)   985 (0/4 off., 10/46 men)
5th Caçadores
   (Lt Col McCreagh)   400 (0/0 off., 5/26 men)
Brigade total   1385 (0/4 off., 15/72 men)

Cavalry (Lumley)

Colonel Otway's Brigade
1st (Alcantara) Dragoons
   (Lt. Col Amoral) – 3 sqns   327 (no casualties)
7th (Lisboa) Dragoons
   (Lt. Col Watson) – 2 sqns   314 (0/0 off., 0/2 men)
5th (Evora) Dragoons
   (Captain Watson) – 1 sqn   104 (no casualties)
8th (Elvas) Dragoons
   (Major Wyndham) – 1 sqn   104 (no casualties)
Brigade total   849 (0/0 off., 0/2 men)

Artillery (Major Dickson)	*Guns*	*Men*
Portuguese Artillery (Braun)	6 x 9 pdrs	221 (0/0 off.,
Portuguese Artillery (Arriaga)	6 x 6 pdrs	2/10 men)

Staff: It is not known how many staff were present but 1 officer was killed and 1 wounded

Total Portuguese casualties – all ranks and arms: 389

SPANISH FORCES
4th Army (Teniente-General Don Joachin Blake)
Vanguard Division (Mariscal de Campo Don José Lardizabal)

Sección de Brig. Joachin Cansinos	Officers	Men
1st Bón Rgto de Murcia (Col. Muñoz)	657[3]	(2/5 off., 26/58 men)
2nd Bón Rgto de Murcia (Col. Muñoz) Bón Fijo Milicia Prov de Canarias[4] (Col Uriundo)	13 (2/4)	420 (16/64)
Sección de Brig. Cesar Gouvea-Cansinos		
2nd Bón, 2nd Rgto de León[5] (?)	19 (0/0)	567 (11/47)
Rgto Ligero de Campo Mayor (Col. Salbany) – 1 bón	26 (0/5)	647 (5/35)
Cazadores Reunidos del Rgto de Murcia	49 (casualties: see main body)	
Division Total	107 (4/13) 2291	(58/204)

3rd Division (Teniente-General Don Francisco López Ballesteros)

Sección de Brig. Clodoveo Gouvea-Asensio	Officers	Men
1st Bón Provisional Compañias de Catalanes[6] (Col Dionisio Vives)	307[7]	(1/1 off., 13/47 men)
Rgto de 2nd Cazadores de Barbastro[8] (Brig. Francisco Merino) – 1 bón (Ligero)	19 (0/2)	546 (5/23)
Rgto de Pravia (Col. Luis Diaz) – 1 bón (Ligero)	31 (0/3)	542 (18/36)
Sección de Brigadier Enrique Carvajal		
Rgto de Lena (Col. Jaime Butler) – 1 bón	28 (1/3)	499 (12/25)
Rgto de Castropol (Col. Pedro Gastelu) – 1 bón	507[9]	(0/2 off., 3/30 men)
Rgto de Cangas de Tineo (Col. Guillermo Livezay) – 1bón	21 (0/1)	559 (2/16)

Rgto de Infiesto (Col. Diego Clarke)
– I bón	19 (2/3)	447 (8/14)
Division total	154 (4/15)	3371 (61/191)

4th Division (Mariscal de Campo Don José de Zayas)

Sección de Brig. Juan de la Cruz Mourgeon	*Officers*	*Men*
2nd Bón Real Guardias de España		
(Brig. Juan Urbina)	24 (0/10)	606 (24/139)
4th Bón Real Guardias de España		
(Col Diego Ulloa)	19 (0/2)	628 (36/130)
2nd Bón Rgto de Irlanda		
(Brig. Ibeagh) – I bón[10]	41 (0/13)	708 (36/223)
3rd Bón Rgto de Irlanda[10]		
(Col Ramon Velasco) – I bón[11]		
Rgto Veteranos de la Patria		
(Col Balanzat) – I bón	28 (0/0)	566 (2/1)
Zapadores (Col Gabrier)		90[12] (no casualties)

Sección de Brigadier Ramon Polo		
Rgto Imperiales de Toledo		
Brig. Davalos) – I bón	28 (0/1)	549 (4/16)
Legión de Vol Estranjeros		
(Col Juan Omlin) – I bón	19 (0/0)	528 (0/19)
Rgto de Ciudad Rodrigo[13]		
(Col Aguila) – I bón	24 (0/0)	423 (0/13)
1st Bón Real Guardias Walonas		
(M-d-C Craywinckel)	18 (0/0)	623 (0/8)
Division total	201 (0/26)	4681 (102/549)

Seconded from 1st Division of 5th Army (Capitán-General Don Xavier Castaños[14])

Sección de Brig. Don Carlos de España (wounded)
Rgto Inmemorial del Rey (Col Berenguer)
  – 1 bón   503 (0/2 off., 0/6 men)
Rgto de Zamora (Brig. Darcourt?)
  – 1 bón[15]   32 (0/0)   312 (0/3)
Rgto Voluntarios de Navarra
  (Col Queri) – 1 bón   861 (0/1 off., 0/18 men)
Zapadores y Guias[16] – 1 compañia   70 (no casualties)
Brigade total   1778 (0/3 off.,
                                 0/27 men)[17]

Cavalry (Lumley)

Brig. Don Casimiro Loy's Brigade (4th Army)	Officers	Men
Esc de Granaderos del IV Ejercito (?)		
– 2 esc	24 (0/0)	260 (1/16)
Escuadron Provisional de Instrucción		
(?) – 1 esc	12 (0/2)	120 (1/10)
Provisional de Santiago[18]		
(Col Sisternes)	30 (0/0)	325 (3/4)
Husares de Castilla (?)	27 (0/0)	367[19] (2/1)
Brigade total	93 (0/2)	1062 (7/31)

Brig. Conde de Penne-Villemur's Brigade (5th Army)
Reales Carabineros de la Guardia
  (Brig. Manuel Marck?)   75 (no casualties)
Rgto de la Reyna (Col Retana)
  – 1 esc   20 (0/1)   118 (5/7)
Rgto de Bourbon (Col Casquero)
  – 1 esc   24 (0/0)   111 (0/0)
Rgto de Lusitania
  (Col Filiberto Mahy) – 1 esc   13 (0/0)   75 (0/0)
Rgto de Algarbe
  (Col Antolin Riguilon) – 1 esc   13 (0/2)   88 (3/4)
Húsares de Extremadura
  (Col Agustin Sanchez) – 1 esc   12 (0/0)   80 (3/3)

Cazadores de Sevilla
   (Col Espinosa) – 1 esc   c.120 (no casualties)
Brigade total   749 (0/3 off., 11/14 men)

Artillery (Col Miranda)
4th Rgto (Miranda's Battery)   6 x 4 pdrs   103 (1/0 off.,
                                             1/7 men)

Staff: 2 killed, 9 wounded.
Total Spanish casualties – all ranks and arms: 1368

Total Allied casualties – all ranks and arms: 5916

THE FRENCH
Commander-in-Chief: Maréchal Jean-de-Dieu Soult, Duc de Dalmatie

V CORPS (GÉN. DIV. BARON JEAN BAPTISTE GIRARD)
1st Division (Gén. Div. J B Girard)

	Officers	Men
Brigade Veilande		
(Gén. Brig. Michel Veilande[21])		
34ᵉ de Ligne		
(Col W Remond), 2ᵉ & 3ᵉ Btns		
(Ch. Btn Cadillon & ?)	23 (4/13) [15]	930 (104[22]/298)
88ᵉ de Ligne (Col Letourneur),		
2ᵉ & 3ᵉ Btns		
(Ch. Btn Dubarry & ?)	21 (0/11) [12]	878 (0/394[23])
Brigade Pepin (Gén. Brig. Joseph, Baron Pepin)		
40ᵉ de Ligne (Col Chasseraux)		
1ᵉʳ & 2ᵉ Btns		
(Ch. Btn Woirol & ?)	35 (4/10) [23]	778 (35/299)
64ᵉ de Ligne (Col Vigent[24]),		
1ᵉʳ, 2ᵉ & 3ᵉ Btns (Ch. Btn		
Astruc, Henry & Prichard)	50 (5/18) [26]	1539 (99/529)
Division Total	129 (13/52[76])	4125 (238/1520)

2nd Division (Gén. Div. Comte Honoré Théodore Maxime Gazan)

	Officers	Men
Brigade Maransin (Gén. Brig. Jean-Pierre, Baron Maransin)		
21ᵉʳ Légère (Col Henri-Jacques-Martin Lagarde) 2ᵉ & 3ᵉ Btns (Ch. Btn Bigot & Coget)	43 (3/13) [13]	745 (61/178)
100ᵉ Ligne (Colonel Quiot) 1ᵉʳ & 2ᵉ Btns (Ch. Btn Lalou & Gaud)	33 (4/10) [20]	705 (50/203)
Brigade Brayer (Gén. Brig. Michel-Sylvestre Brayer)		
28ᵉ Légère (Col Jean-André Praefke) 1ᵉʳ, 2ᵉ & 3ᵉ Btns (Ch. Btn Camus, Gerrain & Dedoual)	62 (7/11) [30]	1305 (53/425)
103ᵉ Ligne (Col Jean-Gerard Bonnaire) 1ᵉʳ, 2ᵉ & 3ᵉ Btns (Ch. Btn ?)	38 (4/13) [18]	1252 (48/222)
Division total	176 (18/47 [81])	4007 (212/1028)

Independent Brigades – Part from I Corps

	Officers	Men
Brigade Godinot (Gén. Brig. Deo Gratias Nicolas Baron Godinot)		
16ᵉ Légère (Colonel Dellard) 1ᵉʳ, 2ᵉ & 3ᵉ Btns (Ch. Btn Gheneser, ?, ?)	49 (2/7) [17]	1624 (39/333)
51ᵉʳ Ligne (Col Louis-Paul Baille) 1ᵉʳ, 2ᵉ & 3ᵉ Btns (Ch Btn ?)	65 (0/0) [0]	2186 (2/1)
Brigade total	114 (2/7[17])	3810 (41/334)

	Officers	Men
Brigade Werlé (Gén. Brig. François-Jean Werlé)		
12ᵉ Légère (Col Louis-Etienne Dulong de Rosnay) 1ᵉʳ, 2ᵉ & 3ᵉ Btns (Ch. Btn Armand, Bernard, Louis)	62 (3/15) [29]	2102 (108/643)

55ᵉ Ligne (Col Henry-Cesar-Auguste Schwitzer) 1ᵉʳ, 2ᵉ & 3ᵉ Btns (Ch. Btn Nevailles, Peteil, ?)	58 (4/6) [14]	1757 (68/273)
58ᵉ Ligne (Col Jean-Baptiste-Henri Legrand) 1ᵉʳ, 2ᵉ & 3ᵉ Btns (Ch. Btn Forcade, de Tracy, ?)	55 (6/17) [24]	1587 (23/282)
Brigade Total	175 (13/38 [67])	5446 (199/1198)

Grenadiers Réunis

Grenadier companies of 45ᵉ, 63ᵉ 95ᵉ Ligne & 4ᵉ Regt d'Infanterie de la Vistule	33 [4/9]	1000 (362²⁵)

Cavalry (Gén. Div. Marie-Victor Nicolas de Fay Latour-Maubourg)

Brigade Briché (Gén. Brig. André-Louis Briché)

2ᵉ Hussards (Col Gilbert-Julien Vinot) – 2 esc	23 (1/3) [5]	282 (4/65)
10ᵉ Hussards (Col François de Laval) – 2 esc (commanded by Desmarets?)	24 (1/4) [7]	238 (3/24)
21ᵉʳ Chasseurs à Cheval (Col Charles Steenhaudt) – 2 esc (commanded by Muller?)	21 (0/3) [5]	235 (3/19)
Brigade total	68 (2/10[17])	755 (10/108)

Brigade Bron (Gén. Brig. André-François Bron de Bailly)

4ᵉ Dragons à Cheval (Col Pierre Joséph Farine) – 3 esc	21 (3/1) [11]	385 (27/39)
20ᵉ Dragons à Cheval (Col Corbineau) – 2 esc	22 (1/4) [12]	244 (6/14)
26ᵉ Dragons à Cheval (Col de Montelegier) – 3 esc	27 (1/2) [3]	394 (5/13)
Brigade total	70 (5/7 [26])	1023 (38/66)

Brigade Bouvier des Eclaz (Gén. Brig. Bouvier des Eclaz)

14e Dragons à Cheval (Col Denis Eloi Ludot) – 2 or 3 esc (commanded by Hudry?)	17 (0/1) [1]	299 (6/17)
17e Dragons à Cheval (Col Frédéric Auguste de Beurman) – 2 or 3 esc	17 (0/3) [6]	297 (12/30)
27e Dragons à Cheval (Col Charles François Antoine Lallemand) – 2 esc	14 (0/3) [5]	235 (2/14)
Brigade Total	48 (0/7 [12])	831 (20/61)

Unbrigaded Light Cavalry

1er Lanciers de la Vistule (Col Jan Konopka) – 4 esc	28 (1/10) [14]	563 (41/78)
27e Chasseurs à Cheval (Col Prosper d'Aremberg) – 3 esc	22 (0/3) [3]	409 (7/16)
4e Chasseurs d'Espagne (Commander: Jacobo Foiret) – 1 esc	195 (0/0 off.,	0/6 men) [3]
Brigade total	1217 (1/13 [20] off.,	48/100 men)

Artillery (Gén. Brig. Charles-Etienne-François Ruty

3e Regt Artillerie à Cheval (Col Louis Dogereau[27]) – 2 compagnies	12 x 6 pdrs	625 (no casualty returns made)
5e Regt Artillerie à Cheval (Col François Beaudouille Berge) – 3 compagnies	18 x 6pdrs	
6e Regt Artillerie à Pied (Col Jean-Edmond Filhol de Camas) – 3 compagnies	18 x 8 pdrs	608 (1/3 [6] off., 19/72 men)

Staff: 5 officers killed, 8 wounded.

Total of the army:[28] per Soult's returns: 5936; estimated by Lapéne and Belmas: 7000.[29]

Appendix 2

Zayas's 'Instrucciones sobre el buen orden militar'

The document shown in the next page is a copy of the first page of Zayas's 'Instrucciones sobre el buen orden militar' from the Spanish Military Archives. It was used to train his and Lardizabal's divisions whilst in the San José Camp on the Isla de León the year previous to the battle.

The document commences: 'The success of every military expedition depends on proper combination and direction by the Commander-in-Chief, helped by the most exact and punctual obedience of the subalterns and the bravery of the troops.' The term 'combination' probably means something like 'consideration of every aspect'. A further 10 pages outline what is expected from every member of a battalion in the Division. It covers use of the bayonet, junior officers not allowing individual soldiers to leave the ranks and a myriad other matters that are essential to battalions behaving in a manner designed to achieve success and avoid disaster. We have not so far been able to translate more than the odd sentence due to the cursive hand used in its writing – probably by one of Zayas's clerks or aides.

El éxito de toda expedición militar depende de la acertada combinación y dirección del Gefe principal, poderosamente auxiliada de la mas exácta y puntual obediencia de los subalternos, y del valor de la tropa. Estas calidades son tan preciosas, que sin ella la actividad y genio de los Capitanes mas experimentados, no sería bastante á contener y disminuir los males que inevitablemente se siguieran de no obrar. Lo que meditamos y debemos executar desde aquí, no es pan sencillo, y exige gran firmeza de ánimo y toda la energía y espíritu de hombres á quienes la idea de la honrosa esclavitud ofenda mas que la muerte: en pues nuestra Patria é obligación inspiran confianza en el que manda, serenidad y grandeza en el ánimo de los oficiales que no hay pérdida que equivalga á la

Appendix 3

Introducción en Español para Sr Jesús Maroto

Una carretera importante, la N-432, lleva a todos los coches que salen de la ciudad de Badajoz por esa vía hasta la cercana localidad de La Albuera. Si el viajero va con prisa, probablemente no se dará cuenta de que a la entrada se halla un mural sobre el que se puede leer el primer verso de un poema de Lord Byron: *Oh Albuera, Glorious Field of Grief!* En el mismo se representa, además, la efigie de cuatro soldados: un español, un británico, un portugués y un francés. Debajo de cada uno de ellos –en el idioma correspondiente a su nacionalidad– continúa la inscripción: *In rows, just like they fought, they lay like hay in the open countryside* . . .

Por otro lado, si el viajero es curioso y recorre su camino con la ilusión de descubrir nuevos lugares, la vista de un mural tan particular seguramente le hará detener su vehículo y adentrarse en las calles del pueblo. En la plaza principal su curiosidad se verá exacerbada al encontrarse con un monumento conmemorativo de la batalla que se libró en los campos cercanos el 16 de mayo de 1811: un pedestal coronado por un busto del general Castaños, el vencedor de otra batalla ocurrida tres años antes, la tan famosa de Bailén. A ambos lados del busto se alzan dos pequeñas columnas sobre cuyas bases aparecen labrados los nombres de varios generales aliados: Blake, Lardizabal, Ballesteros, Zayas, Carlos de España y Penne por parte española; Beresford, Hamilton, Lumley,

Cole, Stewart y Alten por la británica. No es un monumento espectacular, ni siquiera es bonito, por lo que una vez contemplado es fácil que su imagen se desvanezca de la memoria.

Con tiempo, el viajero descubrirá nuevos hitos desperdigados por dentro y por fuera del caserío: un pequeño monolito que recuerda a los oficiales españoles de Estado Mayor caídos en la batalla; otro monolito – bastante más grande y de construcción más reciente – que recuerda a los muertos británicos; un busto del poeta Lord Byron; y, finalmente, un mural fabricado en cerámica en el que se representa un plano descriptivo de la batalla. Además, junto a la iglesia se halla un Centro de Interpretación de la Batalla que, por medio de un diorama y de diversos planos y grabados, da cuenta de todo lo acontecido en los campos de La Albuera ese trágico día de 1811. En las vitrinas, los distintos artefactos encontrados por los campesinos al labrar las tierras – proyectiles, hebillas, botones, fragmentos de sables y mosquetes entre otros producen una sensación de estremecimiento que nos acompaña durante muchas horas después de abandonar el lugar.

Cada año, hacia mediados de mayo, la melancolía deja paso a la algarabía. Varios miles de personas – se han llegado a contabilizar hasta 20.000 – se dirigen a esta localidad pacense para contemplar el espectáculo de la recreación de la batalla. Voluntarios procedentes de distintos países y gran parte de los habitantes de La Albuera se convierten por unos días en soldados de la época de las guerras napoleónicas que desfilan, se tirotean y soportan terribles cargas de caballería, causando el mayor regocijo entre el público asistente. Este acontecimiento –institucionalizado desde 1965 – dura tres días y ha llegado a contar hasta con unos novecientos participantes sobre el campo de batalla. Además, unos trescientos vecinos representan una obra de teatro con el título 'Albuera: historia de amor y muerte', un drama humano en el que personajes de ambos bandos sufren la crudeza de la guerra. Las numerosas personas que presencian todos estos actos pronto se dan cuenta de que aquello no es una fiesta, sino la conmemoración de un hecho del pasado que hizo que este pequeño pueblo de Badajoz entrara en la historia de Europa. Todo el que ha presenciado recreaciones de este tipo conoce perfectamente los objetivo de las mismas: rememorar un pasado de batallas y conflictos para que no se cometan los mismos errores en el presente, fomentar la confraternización entre los pueblos y hacer accesible la historia por medio de la divulgación. Y, por qué no, también pasar unos días de convivencia y diversión con gentes de otros países que comparten la pasión por una época tan apasionante como la napoleónica.

Entre el público, algunos se identificarán con el bando o la unidad que más le fascine. Pero entre los recreadores poco importa que se represente un temible lancero polaco o un soldado del regimiento británico Middlessex, encarnecidos enemigos en la batalla porque, al final de la jornada, todos formarán en el Parque Wellington para rendir homenaje a los caídos de la Batalla de La Albuera.

Ahora bien, a pesar de tan importante conmemoración, es triste reconocer que la cultura popular española sobre la batalla de La Albuera es más bien escasa. Mucha gente sabe que se libraron las batallas de Bailén y Los Arapiles o conoce algo sobre los guerrilleros o sobre personajes tales como Wellington o Castaños. Pero no mucho más, esa es la verdad. Los vistosos uniformes de los participantes y los estruendos que originan las descargas de los mosquetes han de contribuir al conocimiento de la historia propia, y con ello a la valoración del lugar por parte del público que presencia los actos, de tal forma que se cree la necesidad de iniciativas turísticas y culturales para el futuro próximo. El pueblo de La Albuera no posee conjuntos monumentales destacables y el paisaje que ofrecen los campos circundantes carece de atractivo, especialmente si el lugar se visita en los meses de verano. El pasado histórico se convierte, de este modo, en el mejor patrimonio de muchos lugares de España.

Llegados a este punto deberíamos preguntarnos qué representa La Albuera para los españoles interesados en la historiografía de la Guerra de la Independencia. Antes que nada es preciso reconocer que, aunque se han publicado varios artículos en revistas especializadas, no se ha publicado todavía en España un estudio profundo sobre la batalla. En cambio, en el Reino Unido, existen varias obras en el mercado bibliográfico. Usted tiene en sus manos la tercera o la cuarta. En cambio, en nuestro país, hay varios dedicados a Bailén y, en menor cantidad, a las batallas de

Talavera y de Los Arapiles, aparte de obras aisladas dedicadas a las batallas de La Barrosa, Ocaña y Sagunto, y eso que estas dos últimas fueron, como se sabe, dos batallas catastróficas para los ejércitos españoles.

La batalla de La Albuera supone el cuarto hecho de armas en el que participaron como aliados soldados de los ejércitos español y británico. En la primera de las intervenciones conjuntas, los soldados de Sir John Moore se limitaron a observar cómo los restos del ejército del Marqués de la Romana marchaban tras ellos en la trágica retirada hacia La Coruña, para luego terminar perdiéndolos de vista en las sierras de Galicia. Las tropas españolas, integradas por soldados enfermos y malamente uniformados, causaron una pobre impresión a sus compañeros británicos. Se trataba de un ejército español que había sufrido una estrepitosa derrota en la batalla de Espinosa de los Monteros. En un principio lo formaban soldados entrenados, pero tras la debacle y varios días de una infernal retirada por las montañas del norte peninsular, éstos solo pensaban en sobrevivir y en huir lo más lejos posible de la letal caballería francesa. La deserción se convirtió en una verdadera opción frente a una retirada que no se sabía donde terminaba. Además, para terminar de desmoralizar a la tropa, llegaron noticias de que otros dos ejércitos españoles habían sido derrotados en Tudela y Gamonal. Cualquier nación, tras la evacuación de las tropas aliadas británicas por los puertos de La Coruña y Vigo, hubiera pedido la paz porque, técnicamente, España ya había perdido la guerra. Pero los españoles siguieron resistiendo, lo que ofrecería nuevas oportunidades de luchar hombro con hombro con los británicos.

El segundo encuentro tuvo lugar en Talavera. El Ejército de Extremadura, bajo el mando del general Cuesta, se unió al de Arthur Wellesley. La nueva expedición británica y la detención de los franceses en el centro de España reavivaron los deseos de resistencia. Se crearon nuevos ejércitos con los restos de los anteriores y de nuevo los españoles se lanzaron al campo de batalla. Pero la moral no podía ser muy alta entre unos hombres que habían sido derrotados y que habían visto como muchos de sus camaradas desertaban. Además, carecían de entrenamiento. En Talavera, el peso principal del ataque francés cayó sobre las líneas británicas, bien adiestradas y pertrechadas. Al mismo tiempo, entre los españoles, varios batallones de tropas bisoñas huyeron al oír el estruendo provocado por una descarga de mosquetes procedente de su propio bando. Aunque Cuesta castigó duramente, incluso con la muerte, a los fugitivos capturados, la impresión que este episodio causó entre las tropas británicas no pudo ser peor. Si, además de no ser capaces de suministrar comida y medios de transporte al ejército británico, los españoles eran poco fiables en el campo de batalla, la permanencia del ejército británico en España no tenía sentido. Lógicamente, Wellesley decidió retirarse a Portugal para poner a salvo a sus hombres, que ahora se enfrentaban a un avance masivo de tres ejércitos franceses que convergían sobre los aliados. Todo resultó un desastre. La amargura se apoderó del corazón de los oficiales británicos, que se lamentaban por no haber conseguido nada positivo tras aquella campaña, después de tantos sacrificios como habían hecho. Desde su punto de vista, los españoles eran unos cobardes que se aprovechaban de los héroes británicos. En cambio, desde el punto de vista español, los británicos habían abandonado a sus aliados, que quedaban solos frente al imparable avance de ejércitos más numerosos y de mucha mejor calidad.

En el año prévio, el espejismo de Bailén actuó de forma funesta para la Junta Central española, que se creyó capaz de repetir aquella campaña triunfal de 1808 que provocó la evacuación de Madrid por parte de los franceses. El resultado fue muy distinto, porque todo acabó con una gran derrota de los españoles en la batalla de Ocaña. Un desastre de enormes dimensiones que supuso la aniquilación de los Ejércitos del Centro español. España volvía a perder la guerra por segunda vez. Muchos españoles así lo entendieron y dieron un gran recibimiento al rey José en un viaje triunfal por Andalucía. En el sur solo quedaba Cádiz como baluarte de la resistencia y todo indicaba que terminaría rindiéndose al mariscal Victor. La alternativa para muchos soldados veteranos era formar parte de las guerrillas que se estaban creando, lo cual tenía muchas ventajas, tales como la del saqueo indiscriminado o la falta de disciplina militar, además de la posibilidad de luchar cerca de sus hogares. Solo grupos de oficiales del ejército español pensaban que la resistencia a largo plazo podía terminar en un triunfo. Pero éste se veía muy lejano si no se podía contar con la ayuda británica.

De forma sorprendente, la fortaleza de Cádiz resistió al envite francés. Al cabo de cierto tiempo, los británicos decidieron que podía merecer la pena colaborar con los españoles para lograr levantar el sitio al que las tropas del mariscal Victor sometían a la ciudad. Es el tercer intento de colaboración hispano-británico que se materializa en la batalla de La Barrosa o de Chiclana. Esta batalla se libró un año después de iniciarse el cerco de Cádiz. Participaron dos divisiones españolas y una angloportuguesa y la batalla se decidió en favor de los aliados, aunque la victoria se debió en realidad a la división angloportuguesa, que se enfrentó a fuerzas muy superiores. Los españoles no les ayudaron con todas las fuerzas de las que disponían, sino que se limitaron a restablecer la comunicación con la ciudad sitiada siguiendo las disposiciones del general La Peña. Los oficiales británicos acusaron a los españoles de traición y la Junta Central decidió destituir al general español. El resentimiento entre ambas partes se incrementó con este penoso episodio. Los españoles no podían esta vez culpar a los británicos de falta de ayuda, ya que la batalla de La Barrosa mostraba más bien lo contrario. Y lo que es peor, estas tropas españolas sí habían recibido un entrenamiento eficaz. No se trataba de soldados novatos, sino de hombres muy bien adiestrados por los generales Zayas y Lardizábal en el campo de San José. Ese año de 1811 transcurrió con británicos y españoles lanzándose continuos reproches y acusándose los unos a los otros de haber provocado la delicada situación en la que se encontraban. Incompetencia española según los británicos y falta de colaboración según los españoles. Pero quedaba otra cuarta oportunidad de colaboración y esta llegó con La Albuera.

No se puede resumir la batalla que tan magistralmente se describe en las páginas siguientes, que son el fruto de las investigaciones de Michael Oliver y Richard Partridge. Su descripción tan detallada y amena nos vuelve a convertir en espectadores para que nuestra imaginación provea las imágenes de ese acontecimiento. Estas páginas deben leerse como una obra de ficción, porque hay argumento, personajes, héroes, paisaje, sacrificio . . . En resumen, puede decirse que hay una amplia diversidad de relatos y descripciones. Unas nubes provocadas por la pólvora que inundan el campo de batalla; una lluvia que impide identificar donde se encontraban unos y otros; unos jinetes que surgen de la bruma armados con lanzas, que al principio parecían pertenecer a la caballería española y luego resultaron ser los temibles polacos del coronel Konovka . . . Michael Oliver y Richard Patridge han conseguido escribir un gran relato de total fiabilidad histórica.

¿Consiguió la batalla de La Albuera eliminar parte de la incomprensión que existía entonces entre españoles y británicos? Seguramente no. Sherer cuenta que, cuando los hombres de Zayas eran relevados para ir detrás de la 2ª División, 'un noble oficial español cabalgó hacia mi, y me espetó con orgullo y brava ansiedad que se había ordenado a sus campesinos retirarse, pero que no estaban huyendo'. Pasarán todavía dos años hasta que Arthur Wellesley sea nombrado General en Jefe de los ejércitos aliados; en ese lapso de tiempo la falta de comprensión entre las dos partes se irá reduciendo, porque los hechos darán la razón a la paciente táctica del Duque frente a la de los españoles, demasiado ansiosos por liberar a su país de los franceses. España había dejado de perder la guerra. La mirada azul glacial de un Grande de España, Sir Arthur Wellesley, quedó grabada en la memoria de todos los generales españoles que combatieron a sus órdenes. Si contemplamos el retrato que pintó Goya, todavía nos estremece la dureza de su mirada.

Es de agradecer que los autores de este trabajo de investigación hayan tenido en cuenta la documentación recogida en los archivos españoles. Los españoles debemos colaborar con los historiadores británicos dedicados al estudio de la Guerra Peninsular, porque de esta manera podremos comprender cuáles son los diferentes puntos de vista frente a un conflicto de tan difícil interpretación en algunos casos. Esperamos que este libro contribuya a incrementar la colaboración entre historiadores de ambos países, de tal forma que podamos superar viejas rencillas historiográficas y admitir que miles de soldados británicos dieron su vida por la independencia de España. Esta tierra empieza a reconocer los méritos de los aliados británicos con monumentos cada vez más numerosos, pero todavía insuficientes.

La Albuera es solo un principio. Muy cerca están ya las conmemoraciones del bicentenario del comienzo de la Guerra de la Independencia, que esperamos sea muy fructífero.

Notes

FOREWORD
1. A special area used by the villagers to hold meetings and festivals, sometimes related to the battle and sometimes not. It contains several *cantinas* each dedicated to a regiment from the battle and a parade-ground where re-enactors can practise.

CHAPTER 1
1. W E M Napier, *History of the War in the Peninsula* (Constable & Co. 1992), vol. 1, book 3, chs 1–2.
2. Ibid., p. 138.

CHAPTER 2
1. J Zayas, 'Instrucciones sobre el buen orden militar dictadas en el Campo de San José', 1811.
2. C Oman, *A History of the Peninsular War* (Greenhill Books, 1995), vols 1–7, details these and other battles.
3. Ibid., vol. 1, p. 163.
4. Ibid., vol. 4, p. 99 (footnote 2).
5. We have no record of when or where he died any more than we do of the details of his birth or early military career.
6. Much of this background was provided by Jesús Maroto and Alejandro Zurdo. It formed part of a presentation given by them to La Junta Directiva de la Asociación para el Estudio de la Guerra de la Independencia. Sr Maroto gave permission for its use and a considerable amount of assistance in researching Spanish archives and documents.
7. A copy of this document is in the possession of the authors but is written in a very cursive hand and a Spanish palaeographer we consulted was unable to decipher it. We reproduce the first page in Appendix 2.
8. A D Von Schepeler, *Histoire de la révolution d'Espagne et de Portugal*

(Adamant Media Corporation, 2003; Elibron Classics replica of 1829 original), vol. 3, p. 162.

9. M Oliver and R Partridge, *Napoleonic Army Handbook*, vol. 2, *France and her Allies* (Constable & Co. 2002).

10. A reference, apparently, to the heraldic lions on the British royal family's coat of arms which the emperor seems to have mistaken for leopards.

11. M Urban, *The Man who Broke Napoleon's Codes* (Faber & Faber, 2001).

12. A Pigeard, *Les Etoiles de Napoleon* (Edition Quatuor 1996), p. 375 (quoting from Joseph Bonaparte, vol. 7, pp. 14–15, notes), trans. by the authors.

13. Ibid., p. 377 (quoting from Lejeune, vol. 2, p. 86), trans. by the authors.

14. Ibid. (quoting Sébastien Blaze, p. 202).

15. Raised by Charles de Fay in 1765 as the 'Chasseurs de Flandres'.

16. D Smith, *Napoleon's Regiments* (Greenhill Books, 2000), p. 277.

17. There is just a possibility that they were on the far left of 2nd Division, since Lardizabal reports 'a small English battalion' as advancing with some of his troops at the end of the battle, although this is conjecture on our part.

18. I Fletcher, *Galloping at Everything* (Spellmount Publishers, 1999).

19. The troop landed in Portugal in March 1810 but had had to give up some of its equipment to A (the Chestnut) Troop due to sickness. These losses had not been made good by the battle of Albuera.

20. F. Duncan, *History of the Royal Regiment of Artillery* (Murray, 1879; repr. Naval and Military Press, 2006?), vol. 2, p. 296. A. Dickson, *The Dickson Manuscripts* (Woolwich, 1908; repr. Trotman, 1988), p. 535, suggests that all six cannon were present (presumably five 9-pounders and one 5.5 inch howitzer).

21. Properly, the 4th Division got this for their work during the Pyrenees campaign; before that they were called the 'Supporting Division' for their role alongside the 2nd Division.

22. For the interested reader we recommend S G P Ward, 'The Portuguese Infantry Brigades, 1809–1814', *Journal of the Society for Army Historical Research*, LII/214 (Summer 1975).

CHAPTER 3

1. Wellington Despatches, Elvas, 23 April 1811: 'the most . . . advantageous place . . . will be Albuera'.

2. M. Thompson, *The Fatal Hill* (Mark Thompson Publishing, 2002), p. 100.
3. Wellington Despatches, Elvas, 24 April 1811.
4. General Lord Viscount Beresford, *Refutation of Colonel Napier's Justification of his Third Volume* (Mark Thompson Publishing, reprint of 1834 edn.), p. 106.
5. Supplementary Despatches, Valverde, 15 May 1811: Beresford complained to Wellington that he was 'placed in that position that has already made me so uneasy, and from which I have not been able to extricate myself'.
6. Major General Sir B D'Urban, *Report on the Operations of the Right Wing of the Allied Army under Field Marshal Sir Wm. Carr Beresford in The Alemtejo and Spanish Estremadura during the Campaign of 1811* (Mark Thompson Publishing, reprint of 1832 edn.), p. 24.
7. Madden had experienced a severe setback in the Battle of the Gebora three months earlier, although few men were lost, and wrote an inadequate letter to Wellington in mitigation. Beresford sent for him to ride to Albuera but he never appeared and his exact whereabouts have not been established to this day. Oman (*History*, vol. 4, p. 375) says that two of Madden's squadrons were found and joined Otway. Oman suggests that Madden had 'crossed the Guadiana to Montijo'.
8. M Thompson, *The Letters of Long and Beresford* (Mark Thompson Publishing, 1993), C E Long's Reply to Lord Beresford, First Letter, p 81. C E Long was Brigadier Long's nephew and he wrote, in 1833, contesting Beresford's claim in Anon. (D'Urban?), *Further Strictures on those parts of Colonel Napier's History of the Peninsular War* . . . (Mark Thompson Publishing, reprint of 1832 edn.), that his uncle had retreated too rapidly from Santa Marta.
9. D'Urban, *Report of Operations of the Right Wing*, p. 25, from *Further Strictures on those parts of Colonel Napier's History of the Peninsular War* . . . (Mark Thompson Publishing, reprint of 1832 edn.).
10. T H McGuffie (ed.), *Peninsular Cavalry General 1811–1813* (Harrap & Co. 1951), p. 104; this is a commented compilation of Long's letters.
11. A Burriel, *Relación de la Batalla de La Albuhera* (Spanish Archives), p. 12. Burriel was chief of the Spanish general staff. His report included divisional commanders' reports as well as his own.
12. Ibid. (de España's report), p. 12: 'I was appointed by the General in Chief to the division led by General Zayas').

13. *Mémoires du Maréchal Soult (L & A de Saint-Pierre)* (Hachette, 1955), p. 236.
14. Oman, *History*, vol. 4, p. 377, says one brigade of infantry had arrived at the battlefield as darkness fell. This is not at variance with our statement, since the last of the French troops (Werlé's brigade) did not arrive until around 07.30 hours, and Oman acknowledges the main body broke camp merely 'before dawn'.
15. The timings given at the start of each part of the battle are very approximate. The battle certainly started at about 8 a.m. and continued until 2 or 2.30 p.m. Beresford himself states that Zayas held his ground for about an hour and a half, whilst the report submitted by Lardizabal says 'we had been more than two hours suffering the most lethal fire'.
16. 'Meanwhile, the Spanish army [Castaños], coming along the Guadiana by forced marches, managed to reach Albuera in the night . . . we were still unaware of Blake's arrival at the commencement of the attack, the hills and woods having masked his movements.' Soult, *Mémoires*, p. 236. (Trans. by the authors.)
17. Ibid.: 'Il fallait faire vite.' (It was necessary to do it quickly.)
18. Rgto de Campo Mayor and the Cazadores Reunidos.
19. Dickson's estimate of the distance looks a little too high, the modern map and the position of the modern monument, where the battery was sited, in relation to the bridge, indicates about 500 yards. This would have allowed canister to be used on the road on the town-side of the bridge.
20. *Dickson Manuscripts*, vol. 3, p. 395, from a letter written in 1833.
21. Louis-Antoine Gougeat, *Mémoires d'un Cavalier d'Ordonnance du 20e Dragons* (Librairie Historique F Teissèdre, 1997), p. 99. This reference also confirms the appearance of the Vistular Lancers in the vicinity.
22. G Nafziger, M T Wesolowski and T Devoe, *Poles and Saxons of the Napoleonic Wars* (Emperor Press, 1991), p. 110.
23. Von Schepeler, *Histoire de la révolution*, vol. 3, p. 268, footnote.
24. Anon., *Strictures*, p. 151.
25. Beresford, *Refutation*, p. 150.
26. Ibid.
27. Von Schepeler, *Histoire*.
28. 2nd and 4th Reales Guardias de España, Irlanda (from his own division) and Voluntarios de Navarra from de España's division. The small detachment of Zapadores also accompanied this force.
29. Beresford, *Refutation*, p. 150.

30. Von Schepeler, *Histoire*.
31. These were the numbers of battalions which presumably Blake had sent after Zayas to occupy the new line. The identities were, from Ballesteros's Division, 1° de Catalanes, Barbastro and Pravia, and, from Lardizabal's Division, Murcia, Canarias and 2° de León.
32. Zayas and Lardizabal had fought a successful action together the previous year with many of the same units during General Graham's campaign at Chiclana (Barossa).
33. From an official map made by the Spanish Estado Mayor a month after the battle.
34. 2nd and Walloon Guards regiments.
35. It is possible that the ninth battalion was deployed in skirmish order to the front of the formation. J W Fortescue, *A History of the British Army* (reprint by Naval & Military Press, 2004), vol. 3, p. 194, says that the flank columns each comprised one-and-a-half battalions. There were no light infantry regiments in Girard's division but line regiments were theoretically able to break completely into skirmish order. It is equally possible that the skirmish line was formed by detached voltigeur companies from each battalion and that Fortescue's proposition is correct.
36. Burriel, *Relación*, p. 17: 'Ballesteros made the same manoeuvre on the left, keeping two battalions at the rear and firing at everything in sight. He soon attacked the enemy columns on their right flank, containing them and forcing them to cease firing.' The 'same manoeuvre' referred to is advancing in column and deploying the front line to conform with the manoeuvre just carried out by Lardizabal.
37. Zayas's report to the Spanish general staff.
38. An expression which denotes that the companies of a battalion are not deployed in the prescribed manner, with the grenadier company on the right, and the centre companies in numerical order towards the left with the light company taking up the extreme left flank. This situation would have made manoeuvring difficult, uncertain and lengthy – especially under fire or threat from cavalry.
39. There was no order of preference in light battalions and Stewart had previously been in charge of just such a formation.
40. Sir Henry (Harry) George Wakelyn Smith, *The autobiography of Lieutenant-General Sir Harry Smith, baronet of Aliwal on the Sutlej*.
41. Oman, *History*, vol. 4, p. 383, footnote.
42. Soult's army contained a small number of *afrancesado* cavalry which the infantry might have recognized amongst the advancing horsemen.

43. C Oman, *Studies in the Napoleonic Wars* (Methuen, 1929; repr. Greenhill Books, 1987), p. 179 (A Prisoner of Albuera).

44. 'No, sir, but the English are firing into our backs!'

45. Soult, *Mémoires*: 'After this first success, Girard was given the order to turn off to the right towards Godinot. Unfortunately, he believed too soon in the definitive retreat of the enemy: instead of deploying, he continued his movement in column.'

46. Von Schepeler, *Histoire*, p. 273. *Gavachos* was a derogatory term the French used for the Spanish.

47. Anon., *Strictures*, p. 178.

48. Latour-Maubourg's hand-written report to Soult dated 27 May 1811. He does not say which regiments went to the right but this explains why Abercrombie did not move on to Gazan's right flank before Hardinge rode across.

49. Mariscal de Campo Lardizabal, in his report to the general staff, suggests that his battalions exchanged positions with the British troops (presumably of Abercrombie's brigade): 'A change in the two lines was carried out with the silence of a holy service. They [the British] sustained the fire for half an hour with their characteristic perseverance and bravery, and we, passing through their intervals, occupied the front line at the moment when the enemy gave their third charge with all possible strength, desperately, making a last effort to break our line through the centre.' This seems to be timed at the point when General Werlé was killed and so was probably quite late in the proceedings. The Spanish battalions involved in this charging and counter-charging were Murcia, Canarias and León. He also mentions 'a small English battalion on my left'. Could this, we wonder, be the 3 companies of 5/60th? Ballesteros reports similar activities (including bayonet charges) and it seems the British and Spanish repeatedly supported each other in this manner.

50. In Miranda's report to the general staff, he says 'a box of munitions of a limber being destroyed by an enemy shell [we had] to stop the fire for a while because it caused disorder amongst the livestock'. The 'livestock' are recorded by Miranda as being mules.

51. M. Sherer, *Recollections of the Peninsula* (Spellmount, 1996), p. 161: 'A constant feeling to the centre of the line and the gradual diminution of our front more truly bespoke the havock of death.' Sherer served in 2/34th of Abercrombie's brigade but his description would apply equally to the experiences of Hoghton's or Colborne's men.

52. There is a mistaken view that British infantry maintained a rate of fire of three rounds per minute (which the French could not match). The

normal content of a soldier's ammunition pouch was 60 rounds which, at that rate, would have lasted a mere 20 minutes. Fouling of the musket barrel and concerns for how long ammunition would last mitigated against a fast rate of fire – the initial fire fight lasted for some 90 minutes. Generally, the British preferred to hold their fire until the enemy was at point-blank range, fire a single (devastating) volley, give three cheers and level their bayonets, then charge. This was frequently sufficient to panic their opponents into a precipitate retreat. However, such tactics were usually employed in defence.

53. Ibid., p. 160. Again, Sherer's words would describe the experiences of battalions other than his own.
54. Ibid.
55. Lt Col Duckworth of 2/48th died of his wound, whilst Lt Col White (29th) recovered.
56. Oman, *History*, appendix XVI, p. 634 – quoting a return in the Archives de Guerre of 19 July 1811
57. *The Dispatches of FM the Duke of Wellington 1799–1818*, ed. J Gurwood, trans. from the French by D E Graves (Murray, 1837–9), vol. 5, pp. 770–1.
58. Thompson, *Fatal Hill*, p. 132, citing *United Service Journal* (Oct. 1840), 247.
59. Anon., *Strictures*, p. 179.
60. Beresford, *Refutation*, p. 234.
61. We could find no record of whether Roverea succeeded in motivating any Spanish support. Oman, *History*, p. 389, suggests that Roverea received his wound on the way to delivering Cole's request for orders but Thompson (*Fatal Hill*, p. 135), indicates that this was not the case.
62. Thompson, *Fatal Hill*, quoting from *United Service Journal* (April 1841), 540.
63. Ibid.
64. Beresford, *Refutation*, p. 232.
65. Sir A Dickson quoted in Sir W F P Napier's letter to Marshal Beresford in the latter's *Refutation*, p. 32. Dickson says he is unsure which of the two options was included in the order.
66. Latour-Maubourg's report: 'the head of the column penetrated the enemy's ranks'. Latour-Maubourg makes no reference to the regiments in Bouvier des Eclaz's brigade in this charge although other histories suggest they were involved – see Chapter 4.
67. Ibid.
68. Ibid.
69. Oman, *History*, p. 392, quoting Colonel Blakeney of 7th Fusiliers,

indicates 'thirty or forty paces' (about 25–35 yards), whilst Mark Thompson, *Fatal Hill*, p. 139, indicates 'within about 40 yards'.

70. These would be the cavalry mentioned by Sherer as preventing Abercrombie's battalions from effective charges against V Corps (see n. 48 above).

71. Beresford, *Refutation*, p. 238.

72. Soult, *Mémoires*: 'but he [Werlé] was killed as soon as the first volleys [were fired]. This death caused some confusion in his division [*sic*] of which the movement [to support V Corps] remained incomplete.'

73. J S Cooper, *Rough Notes of Seven Campaigns* (Spellmount, 1996; reprint of 1869 edn.).

74. Fortescue, *History of the British Army*, vol. 7, p. 205: '"Stop! Stop the Fifty-seventh," shouted Beresford; "it would be a sin to let them go on".'

CHAPTER 4

1. Supplementary Despatches, vol. 8, p. 133, Beresford to Wellington, 20 May.

2. Gurwood, Despatches, vol. 7, p. 573, Wellington to Beresford, 19 May.

3. Beresford, *Refutation*, p. 150: 'the Spanish armies were not precisely in the same state of discipline as the English'.

4. Anon., *Strictures*, p. 115

5. Fortescue, *History of the Britsih Army*, p. 213.

6. Thompson, *Fatal Hill*, p. 133.

7. Gurwood, Despatches, vol. 7, pp. 588–9, Wellington to Lord Liverpool, 22 May.

8. Oman, *History*, p. 382.

9. Gurwood, Despatches, vol. 7, pp. 599–600, Wellington to Lord Liverpool, 23 May.

APPENDIX 1

1. Each battalion was without one company who fought in Löwe's brigade at Fuentes de Oñoro.

2. Von Schepeler, *Histoire*, vol. 3, p. 273, footnote 2: 'Those [two guns of one of the KGL batteries] were commanded by Lieutenant Scharnhorst, currently a Prussian Major and son of the famous General Scharnhorst . . .' These (we believe from Cleeves's battery) were the first Allied artillery to reach the Spanish hill but were shortly afterwards replaced by Miranda's Spanish guns after 'losing their

officer and nearly all their gunners'. Oman indicates 49 casualties out of 282 effectives from the KGL batteries, so it is possible von Schepeler was exaggerating unless all these casualties were from Scharnhorst's crew.

3. The report of the chief of staff, Burriel, shows this as a single battalion; two battalions were present as a single, combined unit.

4. This was an urban militia garrison battalion and not part of the original Spanish militia.

5. This was the erstwhile militia regiment which, along with the other militia regiments, was taken into the line in 1810.

6. The parent regiment was largely captured and the colonel killed in the fall of Badajoz to the French in March 1811. The survivors re-assembled in Mérida the following month and were formed into a provisional battalion of unknown strength.

7. This, with the figure for Rgto de Castropol at the cue for n. 9, is a balancing figure to reach the reported divisional total. It is assumed that Infiesto would have been stronger than the surviving companies from Catalanes but the split is arbitrary.

8. The Spanish Estado Mayor map shows this simply as 'Balbastro' (incorrect spelling) but the official list of dead and wounded gives the correct spelling.

9. See n. 7.

10. These two battalions may have been amalgamated in view of the low total strength. Only a single battalion is mentioned in Burriel's report.

11. The 'first company of cazadores from Irlanda' is reported by Zayas as having been 'under the command of their intrepid commander lieutenant colonel Ramon Velasco' in his battle report to the chief of staff. It would have been unusual for a Lt Col to command a company so we have deduced that he was the commander of the 3rd battalion of the regiment, ceding overall command to his superior, Brigadier Ibeagh.

12. This is a balancing figure. The Zapadores officer complement is not included in the total of officers but is included in the Division total. The lack of casualties suggests the unit was not directly involved in combat.

13. This was the erstwhile militia regiment which, along with the other militia regiments, was taken into the line in 1810.

14. Resigned to allow Beresford to take command.

15. There were originally three battalions in the old line regiment but much combat, reorganization and recruitment has left it impossible

to determine which battalion fought at Albuera – it was possibly an amalgamation of battalions.

16. The Guias were probably a brigaded group from those battalions who had not reorganized from when each of the four companies of a Spanish battalion contained eight 'chosen men' to act as sharpshooters and guides who scouted ahead of the battalion on its march route.

17. Burriel, in his list of 'Muertos y Heridos', lists a '1° de Cataluña' in de España's division and shows casualties for them. To the best of our knowledge there was no Catalonian regiment in the army other than the Provisional unit in Ballesteros's division. These companies were from 1 Rto. We have therefore assumed an error in the report and placed the casualties with the unit in Ballesteros's division.

18. We believe these men were scheduled to be absorbed into the Rgto del Rey line cavalry but had not been by the time of Albuera.

19. We believe there was a deficiency of 10 horses in this total – not all men could be mounted.

20. It has proved extremely difficult to identify French officers commanding regiments and battalions with any consistency – it is also possible, though less likely, that some brigadiers may be shown in command of the wrong brigades. We apologise for any errors we might have made. Many of the data were taken from Soult's report to Marshal Berthier among other sources. The information for casualties is taken from Oman who, in turn, derives his figures from the French Archives de Guerre of 19 July 1811 and a later list by Martinien. He points out that the former list must be incomplete, since Martinien gives the name and regiment of every officer who was a casualty and has 121 more names on his list. We give Martinien's figures for officers in square brackets but these are not broken down into killed and wounded/missing. Unfortunately, there seems to be no similar definitive list by regiment for other ranks.

21. Veilande was previously Colonel of the 88th Ligne.

22. Includes 'missing' officers.

23. As is fairly obvious, this includes the total of killed.

24. Vigent was mortally wounded at Badajoz three months previously, so it is likely that one of the battalion commanders was in charge at Albuera.

25. The figures for officers are from Martinien. Soult's return showed only 10 killed and wounded. The figure for the men killed, wounded and missing is Soult's.

26. Oman, *History*, vol. 4, p. 367: 'They took five batteries (thirty guns)

with them, to add to the eighteen guns of Latour-Maubourg', which suggests that only the cannon were taken, omitting the normal complement of two howitzers per company. It is likely that Latour-Maubourg had three companies of one of the Horse Artillery regiments. Ibid. 380 confirms the presence of eight companies (batteries) of artillery 'Three batteries of field artillery [6e Regt] belonging to the 5th Corps accompanied the 1st Division; a fourth [5e Regt?], of horse artillery, was with the cavalry which covered the left flank of the column. Two more were in company with Werlé's brigade [3e Regt?]. The remaining two [of 5e Regt?] stopped with Godinot opposite Albuera.' Our distribution of HA companies between the two regiments present is somewhat arbitrary but is based on these statements.

27. Smith, *Napoleon's Regiments*, pp. 296–301. We do not know if any of the colonels were present at Albuera or the identities of the companies and their commanders.

28. The archival total of 5,936 for the army must be short by approximately 2,000 men but we can only give the regimental totals according to the Archives.

29. Oman, *History*, p. 395. Oman, himself, suggests 7,900.

Index

171

Index

Index